ON TO NICOLLET

The Glory and Fame of the Minneapolis Millers

BY STEW THORNLEY
Foreword by Dave Moore

NODIN PRESS
Minneapolis

Library of Congress Catalogue Card No. 87-062569
ISBN 0-931714-90-7

Nodin Press, a division of Micawber's, Inc.
525 North Third Street
Minneapolis, MN 55401
Printed in U.S.A., at Gopher State Litho, Minneapolis, MN

Second Printing December 2000

ON TO NICOLLET

The Glory and Fame of the Minneapolis Millers

On to Nicollet: The Glory and Fame of the Minneapolis Millers was first published by Nodin Press in the spring of 1988. The timing wasn't designed to coincide with the aftermath of Minnesota's first major league world championship in baseball. However, as fans continued to celebrate and savor the Twins' World Series victory, the book provided a fitting reminder of the rich baseball heritage that had been present in the state for more than a century.

In recent years, *On to Nicollet* has become a bit of a collector's item. Since going out of print, the book has been available only through used book dealers and has been quite hard to find. For that reason, I'm grateful to the publisher, Norton Stillman of Nodin Press, for his decision to reprint it (just as I was grateful for his original decision to publish *On to Nicollet*).

In terms of the text, the book required little updating. After all, the team's story essentially ended in 1960. There has been some happy news to report, though, with the induction of two more Millers into the Baseball Hall of Fame – Carl Yastrzemski in 1989 and Orlando Cepeda in 1999.

There's also been a bit of sadness as the roster of Millers and fans who are still living continues to dwindle. No loss has been greater to me than that of the man who wrote the foreword for *On to Nicollet*. Dave Moore – a legend in local television, a consummate baseball fan, and an unfailing source of encouragement and support for aspiring authors – died in 1998. Dave's opening for this book was perfect when he wrote it in the fall of 1987, and it's still perfect more than a dozen years later.

Dave was representative of those who remembered and cared about the Minneapolis Millers. And it's to those who still remember and care that this book is rededicated.

— Stew Thornley
October 2000

Acknowledgments

So many people have assisted me in researching and preparing this history of the Minneapolis Millers that it would be impossible to recognize them all. Still, I will make an attempt at it.

Many thanks to:

My folks, Phyllis and Howard Thornley, for raising me properly – as a baseball fan.

Members of the Society for American Baseball Research (SABR): Bob McConnell, Bob Hoie, Clifton Johnson, Lloyd Johnson, Bob Koehler, Phil Lowry, Joe Overfield, Art Schott, and Bob Tiemann; as well as members of SABR's local Halsey Hall Chapter: Dave Anderson, Gary Clendennen, Shirley Crohn, Glenn Gostick, Alan Holst, Alden Mead, Tom Mee, Dave Moore, Joe O'Connell, Fred Souba, Bob Tholkes, Ted Hathaway, George Rekela, Roger Godin, Don Wiese, and Jim Wyman.

Members of the Minneapolis-St. Paul media, past and present: Tom Briere, Roman Augustoviz, Halsey Hall, Dave Mona and Jay Weiner.

John Duxbury and Stan Isle of The Sporting News.

Bob Jansen of the StarTribune Photo Library.

The extremely helpful staff of the Minneapolis Public Library, especially Elizabeth Fugazzi and Raymond Olson.

The staffs of the Minneapolis, Hennepin County, and Minnesota Historical Societies.

Cindy Kreizer of the American Association.

Minneapolis City Council Member Kathy O'Brien and her staff for their assistance in researching city ordinances that affected baseball in Minneapolis.

The many ex-players (Millers and opponents), managers, umpires, and others who took the time to share their memories: Bill Barnacle, Mrs. Belve Bean, Marv Blaylock, Ted Bowsfield, George Brophy, Pete Burnside, Spud Chandler, Herman "Flea" Clifton, Andy Cohen, Shag Crawford, Otto Denning, Chuck Diering, George "Showboat" Fisher, Fabian Gaffke, Billy Gardner, Angelo Giuliani, Pete Guzy, Bert Haas, Mickey Haefner, Herb Hash, Joe Hatten, Joe Hauser, Carmen Hill, Monte Irvin, Lefty Lefebvre, Ad Liska, Stu "Lefty" Locklin, Hugh McMullen, John Mihalic, Bill Monbouquette, Don Mueller, Rance Pless, Eddie Popowski, Dick Radatz, Mrs. Bobby Rhawn, Oscar Roettger, Russ Rolandson, Larry Rosenthal, Joe Rue, Herb Score, Wally Tauscher, Dave Thomas, Frank Trechock, "Broadway" Charlie Wagner, Wes Westrum, Bill Webb, Don Wheeler, Ted Williams, Al Worthington and Adrian Zabala.

Most of all, the men and women who as participants and spectators made this history happen.

FOREWORD

By Dave Moore
WCCO Television

Now that the rest of the country has discovered that professional baseball is played in Minnesota, and that a major-league team—using a handkerchief for a mascot—has imposed a prolonged state of insanity on its populace, fortuitous that a book such as this should appear as evidence that the roots of the game run deep in our state.

For it is my hope that the young people of today will read this book and understand from it that while travel, communications, and merchandising of yesterday were not the sophisticated conduits that have made baseball a part of the mass culture that it is today, public affection for the minor-league game then was every bit as intense as it is for major-league baseball of today.

"On to Nicollet" was the name given the committee of local businessmen whose responsibility it was to arrange for citizen delegations from Elk River and Melrose and Biwabik to have their "day" at Nicollet Park, the cute little toy field nestled into the corner of 31st and Nicollet in Minneapolis, just across the road from the streetcar barns. Its band-box confines produced for the fans memories that have become every bit as indelible as those that Met Stadium and the Metrodome will have on the aged of tomorrow.

So indelible that some fifty years after the fact, I can tell you that Walter Tauscher's uniform number was 15, Andy Cohen's was 2, Dutch Holland, 9, Fabian Gaffke, 11, Joe Hauser, 7.

This was American Association baseball, Class Triple-A, one of three such minor leagues (the International League and Pacific Coast League were the others) that were the next step up to the majors for many—Williams, Mays, Reese, Slaughter, Campanella, Bauer, Siebert—and the first step down for others—Lonny Frey, Carl Reynolds, Riggs Stephenson, Bert Haas, Rube Benton, Hauser, and Cohen.

The author of this labor of love is a remarkable young man. Although he was just two months old when his beloved Nicollet Park was torn down (replaced by a Norwest Bank Office, in front of which now stands a handsome plaque commemorating the site, and for which he personally raised the funds), you will see that he has embraced its history with an affection becoming one who had lived in it most of his life. Yet he has not allowed passion for his subject to interfere with his respect for the objectivity that is required of the scholar-historian.

As a fellow member of the Society for American Baseball Research (SABR), I have heard Stew speak on this subject as eloquently as he writes about it. He is that august group's resident expert on the matter. His narration on the Junior World Series of 1932 and the ludicrous playoff series with Omaha in 1955 is not only enthralling theatre, but superb journalism.

I don't think it disturbs the credence of authorship to mention that in his formative years Stew Thornley was developing the recognizable tendencies of a flake. Suspicions of this occurred on a June afternoon in 1977. Chicago was the Twins' opponent. Many of the 46,463 present may recall it as the day that that number was the largest ever to witness a regular-season Twins game at the Met, that Rod Carew knocked out four hits to raise his batting average over .400, that the little-remembered Glenn Adams – he of the velvet-smooth swing – set a club record by driving in eight runs, and that the Twins beat the White Sox 19–12 to return to first place in the standings.

The mounting of these dramatic events created such a frenzy of euphoria in the young man, that for release – although he claims it was to satisfy a "dare" by his companions – he climbed the left-field foul pole. To the top. The deafening, admiring applause from the record crowd had no effect on the gendarmes who gathered at the base of the pole awaiting his descent. His japery cost him twenty-five dollars, assessed by the City of Bloomington for – well, it couldn't have been for "disturbing the peace" since there was none of that in the ball park on that day.

The picture of him sitting there atop the foul pole made the front page of the *St. Paul Dispatch* and later the *Minneapolis Star* and the *Chicago Tribune*.

While it's not likely that this exquisite gem of a history will reward Stew with the same kind of attention, it is certain to capture the fancy of all those who share the profound observation of Lawrence Ritter, baseball's pre-eminent oral historian: "The best thing about baseball today is its yesterdays."

TABLE OF CONTENTS

Nicollet Park. *Minnesota Historical Society and Minneapolis Star and Tribune.*

INTRODUCTION

O n to Nicollet!" For over two generations of baseball fans this was the battle cry that signalled the return of spring to Minneapolis and the opening of another season of baseball at Nicollet Park.

The history of minor-league baseball in Minneapolis is not the story of one team, but, rather, a number of different teams, playing in a variety of leagues, all performing under the name of the Minneapolis Millers.

During the years the Millers played, they were the only game in town. In the first half of this century only ten cities in North America had major-league baseball; it was no dishonor for a city to be represented by a minor-league team, particularly when the league in which the team played was only a spitball-and-a-holler away from the majors.

The Millers played in such a league, the American Association, during a time in which the minor leagues were more than merely a stepping stone to the next-highest level. Many players were able to earn a comfortable living spending their entire career in the minors.

In the days of the Millers, minor-league fans not only had the chance to see young stars on their way up, but also many veterans who, unlike their modern counterparts, could not afford to retire after their talents began to desert them. As a result, players often hung on as long as they could in the minors, performing the only real skill then, knew-throwing and hitting and catching a baseball.

Minneapolis fans even witnessed seventeen men who once wore a Millers' uniform who are now members of Baseball's Hall of Fame. (Each of the Hall of Famers is noted in the book, and a complete list appears in the Appendix.) And of the fifteen best all-time minor-league players, as selected through a survey of Society for American Baseball Research members in 1983, six are former Millers: Buzz Arlett, Nick Cullop, Spencer Harris, Joe Hauser, Frank Shellenback, and Perry Werden.

Today minor-league franchises, with few exceptions, are either owned or controlled by a major-league team, who routinely jockey players about through their stable of farm clubs. As far back as 1958, *Minneapolis Tribune* columnist Dick Cullum lamented the passing of an earlier era when he wrote, "It was different then because (minor-leagues) clubs were home-owned and owners owned their players outright. A man would play for the same city for many years and would be wholly identified with that city, forming loyalties beyond what can be expected of a come-and-go player of farm-system days."

Why would a person who was born barely two months before Nicollet Park closed be interested in a team he never seen play? That's a question I've often been asked, and I find it a curious one since no one considers it odd that I have an interest in World War

II and the Civil War, even though I wasn't in the bleachers for those events, either.

But my interest in the Minneapolis Millers came from hearing stories of the team from my dad, Howard Thornley, and my grandma, Marie Hubbard. Pa became a Millers' fan during the thirties and then worked as an usher at Nicollet Park and Met Stadium, where the Millers later played. My grandma lived at 36th and Nicollet, just a short stroll from the front gate of the park, where she was a frequent visitor.

In 1937 my grandma stayed at the same hotel with the Millers in Kansas City and collected two pages of autographs. Thirty years later she gave them to me. On those two pieces of paper were scrawled the signatures of Donie Bush, Andy Cohen, Spencer Harris, Fresco Thompson, Fabian Gaffke, Ralph "Red" Kress, Wally Tauscher, and Belve Bean. I had never heard of any of those men—but I would.

I looked up each of their records in my Baseball Encyclopedia. Frequently I sent questions to Halsey Hall, the area's eminent baseball historian; Halsey never failed to return an answer. Over time I had the chance to correspond with a number of those players, and I remember the special kick I felt when I met Fabian Gaffke in Milwaukee in 1983. (Fabian was seventy at the time, but still looked limber enough to patrol center field.)

In the last eight years I've accelerated my research on the Millers and, among other things, have pored over the box score and newspaper account of every game the Millers played since the 1880s. Its been said that researching is like mining: you move a lot of dirt to find a little gold. What follows, I hope, is the gold.

Halsey Hall.

IN THE BEGINNING

The roots of baseball in Minneapolis and the surrounding area are part of the post-Civil War baseball boom in America. The city's earliest team dates back to 1867 with the Minneapolis Unions, an aggregation of prominent young men whose fathers were distinguished members of the municipality. The local version grew in tandem with the wider popularity of the game as it strove to become our national pastime. Through the sixties and seventies the city was represented by different nines with a variety of colorful nicknames, ranging from "Browns" to "White Shirts" to "Blue Stockings" (which followed the custom of the time for a team to derive its nickname from the color of its uniforms).

The moniker "Millers" did not arrive until 1884 when Minneapolis formed its first professional team as a member of the Northwestern League, a minor-league made up of eight teams in Wisconsin, Michigan, Illinois, Indiana, and Minnesota, which, besides Minneapolis, was represented by teams in St. Paul, Stillwater, and later in the season, Winona.

Ben Tuthill, who would later become prominent in the theatrical world, served as manager of the Minneapolis entry. In forming the team, he and owner Joe Murch (a bartender at the Nicollet House) eschewed local talent, opting instead for "real ball players", causing a trio of Mill City stars, Billy O'Brien, Charley Ganzel and Elmer Foster, to cross the river and join manager A. M. Thompson's St. Paul team. (Foster "Babe" Ganzel, the son of Charley and a namesake of Elmer Foster, Charley's best friend, would star at third base for the Minneapolis Millers fifty years later.)

The first meeting between the Twin City rivals in 1884 took place June 23 at the West Seventh Street Grounds in St. Paul before 4,000 fans. Many in that throng were Minneapolitans, loaded with money, offering attractive odds to anyone wanting to bet on St. Paul; they had no trouble finding takers. With Foster on the mound and Ganzel behind the plate, St. Paul shut out Minneapolis, 4-0, as the "real ball players" were unable to get a runner past second base.

Minneapolis did not fare well that year, nor did the rest of the league. Beset by financial difficulties, the Northwestern League folded in early September. Two of its teams joined and finished the year in the Union Association, a major league in its only season of operation. One of the two new teams was St. Paul, giving Minnesota its first representation in major-league baseball. Area fans showed little interest, particularly since the team played all of its Union Association games on the road, compiling a record of two wins, six losses, and one tie during its brief fling in the big time.

Minneapolis continued to be represented in organized baseball—in the resurrected Northwestern League and its replacement, the Western Association—but enjoyed little success until it posted its first winning record in 1889. This was also the Millers' first year in Athletic Park, which was located behind the West Hotel at Sixth Street and First Avenue North (on the current site of Butler Square). The bandbox created some high home run totals even in this era of the dead ball. So small was the new park that players had to frequently "leg out" base hits to right field, and it wasn't uncommon for a runner to be thrown out at first on an apparent single to right. Snug in their new home, the Millers finished third with a 66-56 record.

Their first bona fide pennant race came the follow-

Athletic Park c. 1890. *Minnesota Historical Society.*

ing year with a team many old-timers remember as the best that ever played in the Flour City. With ten straight wins, the Millers held first place by five games following a Fourth of July doubleheader, when two of their star players, centerfielder Elmer Foster and second baseman Moxie Hengle, jumped the club. Without this duo, the burden of holding the top spot for the final two-and-a-half months of the season fell on their spectacular, but sometimes erratic, southpaw hurler, Martin Duke. Down the stretch Duke was magnificent, winning twelve of thirteen games. On September 17 he beat Denver, 3-2, striking out 18 of the Mountaineers. That performance gave him 288 strikeouts (in 274 innings pitched), tying the Western Association record set the year before by Kid Nichols. More significantly, the win put the Millers one-half game ahead of Kansas City in the battle for first place, with a three-game showdown between the two teams set to start three days later. Duke pitched the series opener, but the Kaycee fans had come equipped. Duke's real name reportedly was "Duck," about which he was sensitive. It couldn't have helped his concentration as fans blew duck calls and, in the fourth inning, a live duck was thrown onto the field. Whatever the reason, Duke was as ineffective as he hadn't been in months. The Cowboys beat him again two days later, completing a three-game sweep, and held their margin through the final week of the season.

In 1891 the Millers found themselves in first place in a sudden way. Milwaukee held the lead in mid-August when the Cincinnati franchise in the American Association (in its final year as a major-league) suspended operations, and Milwaukee's Western Association team was offered the chance to complete Cincinnati's schedule. The Brewers accepted the offer and dropped out of the Western Association. Their departure left the Millers in first place with a record of 58-44. The glory was fleeting, however, as only three days later the Millers disbanded because of financial problems, leaving Minneapolis without professional baseball.

To fill the void, Milwaukee's new big-league team transferred its final series of the season, against Columbus, to Athletic Park in Minneapolis. Unbaseball-like weather prevented two of the games, but on October 2, 1891, despite heavy clouds that threatened rain or snow, Minnesota hosted its first—and until the Minnesota Twins arrived, its only—major-league game as Milwaukee beat Columbus, 5-0. The Brewers' Frank (Red) Killen, who had started the season with Minneapolis and had hurled a no-hitter for the Millers the year before, held the visitors scoreless on six hits.

Thus the first decade of baseball in Minneapolis was marked by unstable teams playing in even more unstable leagues. Since the demise of the American Association in 1891, the National League stood alone as baseball's only major league.

But in 1894, Ban Johnson, a Cincinnati sports writer, appeared on the stage of organized baseball. With his friend, Charles Comiskey, manager of the Cincinnati Reds, Johnson revived the Western League in the hopes of transforming it eventually into a major circuit to challenge the National League. Minneapolis was one of the members of the new league.

The first year of the new Western League also marked the debut of Perry "Moose" Werden into lo-

Spectators at Athletic Park c. 1892. *Minnesota Historical Society.*

cal society, where he remained a familiar figure until his death forty years later.

Werden's career had begun as a pitcher with St. Louis of the Union Association in 1884, but he turned his attention to hitting, playing with the famous Baltimore Orioles teams that included John McGraw, Wee Willie Keeler, Hughie Jennings, and Wilbert

Robinson. Moose had already established his slugging reputation when he came to Minneapolis, and he stayed on friendly terms with the fences at cozy Athletic Park, posting home run totals of 42 and 45 in his first two seasons, the latter figure remaining an organized baseball record until Babe Ruth took up the practice. Even after his days with the Millers, Werden spent the off-season in Minneapolis and continued to live in the city following his retirement from baseball. For many years he owned and managed a local independent team known as "Werden's All Stars." Werden died in 1935.

Werden wasn't the only heavy hitter on the team; the mighty Millers averaged over ten runs scored per game in 1894 and 1895. However, their pitchers were equally adept at giving up runs, and the Millers finished no higher than fourth either year.

The frequent parades across home plate might have continued indefinitely, but in May of 1896 the Millers were given their eviction notice from Athletic Park. The land on which their grounds stood, only one block from the main street of Minneapolis, had been sold and they were given thirty days to find a new home. On May 23rd, the Millers played their final game at Athletic Park, then left on an extended road trip, not knowing where their new home would be when they returned.

A. M. Smith's "Bird's Eye View" of Minneapolis includes Athletic Park. *Bob Tiemann.*

Opening Day Ceremonies at Nicollet Park c. 1925. *Minnesota Historical Society.*

ON TO NICOLLET

When the Millers left Athletic Park and embarked on their journey through the eastern cities, four sites were under consideration for their new park, with a location along Kenwood Boulevard, across Hennepin Avenue from Loring Park, being considered the favorite. The city council, however, refused to vacate certain streets in the Kenwood area, and in late May, after the street-car company announced it could better service a park near Lake Street, the decision was made to locate the field at 31st Street and Nicollet Avenue. The ground was quickly graded, bleachers, grandstands, and fences hastily erected, and within three weeks the field was ready for baseball.

All that remained for the wooden structure was a name. Three Minneapolis newspapers invited readers to submit suggestions; from that list a panel of writers selected the name Wright Field, in honor of Harry Wright, one of baseball's founding fathers. The name did not receive a warm reception from the Millers' owners though, and for the next year the stadium was referred to merely as the "new ball park." It wasn't until 1897 that the name Nicollet Park was first used.

The new grounds opened June 19, 1896 as the Millers came from behind to defeat Milwaukee, 13-6. Varney Anderson held the Brewers to eight hits while the Millers' Charley Frank hit the game's only home run—a two-run shot over the right-field fence in the sixth inning.

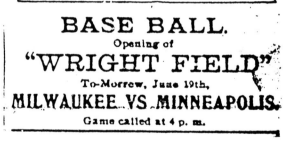

BASE BALL.
Opening of
"WRIGHT FIELD"
To-Morrow, June 19th,
MILWAUKEE VS MINNEAPOLIS.
Game called at 4 p. m.

Advertisement in June 18, 1896 Minneapolis Tribune.

The Millers took a liking to their new playground and moved up quickly in pursuit of their first pennant. Werden's home run total dropped sharply in the more spacious setting on Nicollet, but he still managed 18 round-trippers for the season while hitting .377.

At the helm in his first season as player-manager was Midwest-native Walter Wilmot, who, the preceding six years, had been the highest-paid player in the National League, drawing as much as $4,250 a season while playing for the Chicago White Stockings under Pop Anson (who was paid only $2,000). Wilmot would later coach the Minnesota Gopher baseball team.

Wilmot still had his skills as a ball hawk in left field, and his batting eye remained sharp enough to lead the team with a .391 average.

The Millers remained in the thick of the race until early August when they made their move with an 11-game winning streak. After a loss to Kansas City, they rattled off 19 more wins, then coasted the rest of the way, taking the Western League flag by nine games over Indianapolis.

Righthander Bill Hutchison, who had won 122 games over a three-year span for Chicago in the early 1890s, led the Miller moundsmen with a 38-13 record.

So impressive were the team's exploits that National League clubs plucked away most of their stars for 1897 and the Millers plummeted to the cellar. The most notable player taken was Werden, who would spend his final season in the major leagues with Louisville.

The Millers were still struggling to rebuild in 1898 when their pitching staff was seemingly bolstered by the arrival of a nineteen-year-old righthander, Roger Bresnahan. Bresnahan had posted a 4-0 record for the Washington Senators in 1897. After holding out for more money the following spring, he left Washington, pitched briefly in his hometown of Toledo and then, after a three-month layoff, joined the Millers for whom he pitched in three games. The official records don't even list Bresnahan as having been with Minneapolis in 1898. Bresnahan probably wouldn't have minded the oversight; he was the losing pitcher in all three games he pitched.

Bresnahan was back with the Millers in spring training the following year and even started the team's opener. But for Roger in 1899, once again, it was three games—three losses.

Apparently soured by his mound experience, Bresnahan turned his attention to the other end of the battery, catching fifteen years for the Orioles, Giants, Cardinals, and Cubs, and compiling a .279 lifetime batting average. He was elected to the Hall of Fame in 1945, only a few months after his death.

In 1900 Ban Johnson was at last ready to challenge the National League on an even footing, changing his circuit's name to the American League. Even with the new name, which reflected a more national rather than regional structure, it remained a minor league as part of the National Agreement. That changed the next year as war broke out between the leagues. Meeting overwhelming success in its raids on National League rosters, the American League reached parity with astonishing rapidity. The Twin Cities, however, were left behind. Following the 1899 season, Charles Comiskey moved his St. Paul Saints to Chicago, where they remain to this day as the White Sox. Minneapolis was among a number of cities abandoned after the 1900 season, to be replaced by teams in larger, Eastern cities.

But in 1902 a new minor league was born. The American Association (no connection to the major league of the same name, which had operated from

1882 to 1891) was founded by Thomas J. Hickey and embraced many of the cities that had been part of the Western League in the 1890s. Both Minneapolis and St. Paul were charter members of the new association. Walter Wilmot and Perry Werden returned to the Millers (Wilmot as player-manager), although both were past their prime. In their maroon and blue uniforms, the new Millers (who were also called the "Reds" in their early years) finished in seventh place, 41 1/2 games out of first, and capped their season by being swept in a tripleheader against Indianapolis.

Their neighbors to the east did better. Managed by Mike Kelley, who also played first base in an infield that included future Hall-of-Famer Miller Huggins at second, St. Paul won pennants two of their first three years in the Association. For the Millers, though, things would get worse before they got better.

They lost their first 11 games of 1903 and again finished seventh, this time only one game out of the cellar. Wilmot resigned as manager early in May, with catcher George Yeager taking over the reins.

The Millers finally gained respectability in 1904 and 1905 when W. H. Watkins, owner of the Indianapolis club, purchased the Millers from Clarence Saulpaugh and took over as owner-manager. (Joint ownership of clubs was not unusual during this period. At the same time Watkins controlled Indianapolis and Minneapolis, George Tebeau owned both the Kansas City and Louisville teams.)

Although not a serious contender for the flag, the Millers under Watkins did climb to the first division. With a solid infield of Jerry (Buck) Freeman at first, Billy Fox at second, Andy Oyler at shortstop, and Ed (Battleship) Gremminger at third, they had the nucleus for a winning tradition. Davy Jones, who would

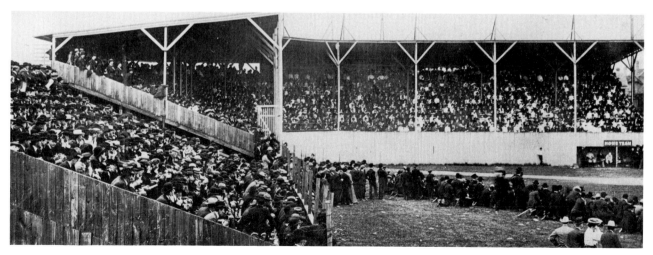

Opening Day at Nicollet Park, 1903. *Minnesota Historical Society.*

Front: Lefty Craig; Peaches Graham; Denny Sullivan; Arthur (Cy) Coulter, W. H. Watkins, Mgr.; Capt. Billy Fox; Andy Oyler; Jess Stovall; Davy Jones.
Back: Clarence Villeman; Charlie Schmidt; Charlie Jaeger; Patsy Hynes; W. H. (Father) Marshall; Bill Chappelle; Otto Newlin; Charlie Sievers; Ed (Battleship) Gremminger; Jerry Freeman.

1905 Millers. *Minnesota Historical Society.*

later roam the Detroit outfield between Ty Cobb and Sam Crawford, hit .346 for the Millers in 1905 to finish second in the Association batting race.

The 1905 Millers had a long list of wounded, including outfielder Cy Coulter, who missed several games and nearly lost his eyesight after mistaking acid for eye wash. His plight, however, was nothing compared to that of the Louisville Colonels, who lost most of their team in August when their wagonette was struck by a trolley car in Kansas City. Although none of the injuries were fatal, they were severe enough to sideline many of the players for the rest of the season. A call went out among the other Association clubs to loan the Colonels players, and Louisville was able to continue with new recruits.

The Millers closed 1905 with high hopes for the coming season, unaware that what lay ahead would be the most volatile year in the history of Minneapolis baseball.

Near the end of the 1905 season Mike Kelley had a falling out with St. Paul owner George Lennon and, around Christmas time, changed his workplace to the other side of the Mississippi River. With some of his own money, and the backing of several prominent local men, Mike became president and manager of the Millers as Watkins returned to Indianapolis.

In the meantime, the Saints had sold Kelley's contract to the St. Louis Browns of the American League, a sale that started a string of controversial incidents involving Kelley in 1906. A faction within the American Association, headed by George Lennon, tried to keep Kelley out of the league by claiming he was now the property of the Browns and not Minneapolis.

Lennon's cabal was successful—at least for one game—as Kelley stayed off the bench for the Miller's 1906 opener in Louisville, at the request of the National Commission (Organized Baseball's governing body.) The next day Kelley moved from the grandstand to the dugout and refused to leave the bench, prompting umpire Brick Owens, acting upon orders from league president Joseph D. O'Brien, to forfeit the game to the Colonels.

Kelley's status was eventually cleared up by the National Commission, and he was allowed to manage the Millers; stormier clouds, however, were beginning to form.

In mid-June Kelley lodged charges against Owens and fellow arbiter Steve Kane, claiming that the duo had deliberately tipped off Louisville batters of the battery signals of his club during a recent series with the Colonels. President O'Brien immediately suspended Kelley, Kane, and Owens pending an investigation. Faced with an order to "put up or shut up," Kelley backed down and denied ever having made charges reflecting upon "the honesty or integrity of the umpires."

The next time Owens umpired a Minneapolis game was July 18. The Millers were riding a ten-game winning streak and had climbed to third place as they opened a four-game series at home with the league-leading Columbus Senators. A close call at the plate by Owens in the eighth inning went against the Millers, sending the game into extra innings. After the Millers lost in the twelfth, hundreds of fans swarmed onto the field in pursuit of the man they held accountable for the defeat. Owens ducked into the visitors' bench and took cover beneath the stands. Police tried to escort Owens from the field but were forced back by the mob. As the crowd grew thicker and surlier, Pudge Heffelfinger, the former All-American guard at Yale and a Minnesota native, worked his way through the crowd, took Owens by the arm and started for the street. According to the *Minneapolis Tribune*, "The stone throwing continued, altho (sic) there was a general recognition of 'Pudge' and a seeming reluctance to bounce any paving material off his head."

A full house was on hand the next day, most of the fans coming equipped with eggs and other projectiles. One man even brought a crate of eggs and stood on the corner of 31st and Nicollet, handing them out to fans entering the grounds. Owens, against the advice of Minneapolis police, took the field but was able to call only one pitch before the eggs started flying. Owens fled the field, forfeiting the game to the Senators. Those two games started a four-game Columbus sweep that effectively ended any Miller hopes of capturing their first American Association flag.

A week later, Miller team secretary, L. A. Lydiard, charged that Owens had placed a bet with local gamblers on the Senators in the July 18 game. Owens was quickly exonerated by league directors, who then set about to determine the parties responsible for the charges. The fingers ended up pointing at Kelley, and, on August 12, Mike was suspended indefinitely by President O'Brien. In addition, a number of Millers players were suspended for their parts in the July 18 riot.

Captain Billy Fox directed the team for the rest of the season. Kelley remained out of the American Association until the owners voted in August 1908 to reinstate him; at that time, Mike took over as manager, once again, of the St. Paul Saints.

THE CANTILLONS

Attendance at Nicollet Park declined sharply following the suspensions of Kelley and the players, and on August 22 the Millers were sold to Gus Koch of Milwaukee. Koch had purchased the team as an investment, but quickly tired of paying salaries and other expenses and watching the crowds become slimmer and slimmer. That winter, Michael E. Cantillon, who had been successful as owner and manager of the Des Moines club in the Western League, approached Koch with an offer to buy. Happy to be rid of the mess, Koch let Cantillon have the franchise and players for $27,500. (The property would reportedly have been a bargain at $150,000.) Mike Cantillon, with his brother Joe and their brother-in-law, E. J. Archambault of Milwaukee, became partners in the ownership of the club and a new era was opened. Mike's first choice as field manager, however, was unavailable, as brother Joe had just signed a three-year contract to manage the Washington Senators. Instead, Mike directed the team from the bench his first two years. The 1907 team featured three players named Freeman, all nicknamed "Buck," one of whom (first-baseman John Freeman) set a new Association record with 18 home runs. The pitching staff was led by Ole Kilroy, a lutefisk manufacturer from Lindstrom, Minnesota, who twice during the season pitched an entire doubleheader.

In 1908 Rube Marquard tuned up for his Hall of Fame career with the New York Giants by winning 28 games for Indianapolis. Minneapolis was one of Rube's favorite targets as he beat the Millers five times during the year, three times shutting them out.

The following season Mike Cantillon decided to concentrate his duties on the front office, so he found a man who would not only manage the team, but hold down the hot corner, as well. Jimmy Collins had hit only .217 for the Philadelphia Athletics in 1908 and was released when Connie Mack decided his salary

Top: Wheeler; Fritz Buelow; Fred Olmstead; Tony Smith; Andy Oyler. *Middle:* Byers; Jimmie Block; Mike Cantillon, Mgr.; Lee Quillen; *Bottom:* Tip O'Neill; Big Bill Clarke; Kerwin; Lou Fiene.

1908 Millers. *Minnesota Historical Society and Minneapolis Journal.*

was too big for his worth to the A's. However, Collins rebounded as manager-third baseman for the Millers. He had to leave the team for a week in May when his nine-month old child died in Buffalo, New York, but came back to hit .273 and lead the Millers in their first real run at the pennant.

Collins, who had a .294 lifetime average in 14 major-league seasons before coming to Minneapolis, was enshrined in the Hall of Fame, along with Roger Bresnahan, in 1945.

Also in 1909 Sunday baseball was played at Nicollet Park for the first time. In the past the Millers had either not played home games on Sunday or had played in other parks, apparently because of local blue laws in effect at that time. However, a check of Minneapolis City Council proceedings reveals that an 1887 ordinance specifically exempted baseball from the list of recreational activities that were outlawed on the Sabbath. Whatever the reasons, since 1894 the Millers had been playing their Sunday home games in White Bear Lake and later at Minnehaha Park, on the southeast corner of East 36th Street and 34th Avenue South.

That summer, fans witnessed the greatest single-day mound performance in the history of the Millers. Tied for first with Milwaukee, Minneapolis faced the Brewers in a doubleheader at Nicollet Park July 13. Irving (Young Cy) Young held the Brewers to four hits in the first game to win, 1-0. Young also homered in the fifth for the game's only run. So impressive was Young that Collins stuck with the southpaw in the nightcap; this time Young Cy held the Brewers hitless until the ninth, finishing with a one-hitter and 5-0 victory. The double shutout put the Millers two games in front of Milwaukee. The two teams scraped

for the lead the next two months, but both faded in the final week, allowing Louisville to sneak into first as the season ended.

Despite the disappointing finish, during the season the Millers acquired three players who would play major roles in the future of the team: Gavvy Cravath came to Minneapolis in June; outfielder Otis Clymer and pitcher "Long" Tom Hughes were obtained from Washington later in the season.

Following the 1909 season, Jimmy Collins left Minneapolis to become manager of the Providence team in the Eastern League, and "Pongo" Joe Cantillon was signed by his brother to manage the Millers.

A native of Janesville, Wisconsin, Pongo was a familiar face in the Upper Midwest. He had played with many teams in the area, including Winona in 1884, in a career that had begun in 1879. He received his nickname when he was a member of the San Francisco Seals in 1889. Cantillon was popular with the Bay Area fans, and Charley Dryden, a baseball writer and humorist of national renown, had received many inquiries regarding Joe's nationality. Dryden wrote that Cantillon was Italian and his true name was Pongo Pelipe Cantillon, son of a nobleman who had run away from his home in Italy to seek his fortune in America. Italian residents took Dryden seriously and went to the park in droves to cheer their countryman. They would yell to Joe in Italian and the young second baseman answered back in guttural tones so natural that even his teammates wondered if Dryden's story was true. (It wasn't.)

As a Western League umpire in the late 1890's, Cantillon was often a favorite scapegoat among Minneapolis sportswriters, and as a scout, Joe was credited with discovering some of the game's

27

greatest players, including Walter Johnson, Rube Waddell, and Amos Rusie. He managed the Milwaukee Brewers in the American Association for four years before signing a managerial contract with the Washington Senators. That commitment now complete, he was ready to join his brother in pursuing a pennant for Minneapolis.

With Mike in the front office and Joe on the bench

Millers vs. Saints at Nicollet Park, 1909. *Minnesota Historical Society.*

and a roster comprised almost entirely of players with previous major-league experience, the Millers rattled off three-straight pennants starting in 1910.

Minneapolis again boasted the Association's premier infield with Warren (Doc) Gill at first, Jimmie Williams at second, "Daredevil" Dave Altizer at short, and Hobe Ferris (an early author of the "tape-measure home run") at third. The outfield combined speed and power with Tip O'Neill (the Association batting champ in 1909) flanked by Cravath and Clymer. Had runs-batted-in been an official statistic at that time, Cravath undoubtedly would have won the Triple Crown in 1910 and 1911. As it was, Clifford Cactus Cravath, home-run king of the dead-ball era, led the league both years in batting average, hits, doubles, home runs, and total bases. In 1911 he hit .363 while pounding 29 home runs, eclipsing by eleven the league record set by John (Buck) Freeman in 1907. (As prodigious as he was with the lumber during his baseball days, Gavvy Cravath later struck out as a judge in Laguna Beach, California when it was discovered that he couldn't hit a scofflaw's pocketbook as well as he could a curveball. A member of the clergy, convicted of speeding, received only a token fine from Cravath, which he then suspended because "A minister must need the money more than the city of Laguna Beach does." Finding Gavvy too soft-hearted to be a good fine collector, the city eventually removed him from the bench.)

Otis Clymer led the league in runs scored in 1911 and 1912, crossing the plate 149 times in 1911 while also setting a league record with a 28-game hitting streak. In addition to being one of the best shortstops in the league, Dave Altizer was also the Association pacesetter in stolen bases two of those pennant-winning years. In 1910 the Daredevil led the league in runs scored and had 61 sacrifices, a record that still stands.

But offense was not the only strong suit of the Millers, as they produced the league's winningest pitcher all three years. Tom Hughes set a record with 31 wins in 1910, Roy Patterson had 24 the following year, and Fred Olmstead won 28 games in 1912. The team also set a still-existing record with 292 stolen bases in 1912. The Millers had no serious challengers for the title those three years, averaging more than 103 wins per season.

The Millers championship teams included two pitchers who would end up in the Hall of Fame.

Twenty-two-year-old righthander Urban "Red" Faber appeared in five games with the Millers in 1911, posting a 1-0 record (although the official record books incorrectly list him as pitching in only two games, without a decision.) After two more stops in the minors, Faber moved to Chicago, where he won 254 games with the White Sox. He was elected to the Hall of Fame in 1964.

Rube Waddell pitched for the Millers in 1911 and 1912, compiling records of 20-17 and 12-6, respectively. Waddell, the premier southpaw of his era (and called the greatest pitcher of all time by Cy Young), had led the American League in strikeouts from 1902 through 1907 while pitching for the Philadelphia Athletics. As eccentric as he was brilliant, Rube withstood all attempts by manager Connie Mack to keep his mind on baseball.

According to Lee Allen in his book, *The American League Story*, Waddell could find much more than just pitching to occupy his time: "Consider merely a few of the things that happened to him in one year alone, 1903: He began that year sleeping in a firehouse at Camden, New Jersey and ended it tending bar in a saloon in Wheeling, West Virginia. In between those events he won 22 games for the Philadelphia Athletics (even though he didn't bother to hang around for the final month of the season), played left end for the Business Men's Rugby Football Club of Grand Rapids, Michigan, toured the nation in a melodrama called 'The Stain of Guilt', courted, married and became separated from May Wynne Skinner of Lynn, Massachusettes, saved a woman from drowning, accidentally shot a friend through the hand, and was bitten by a lion."

When Waddell joined the Millers in 1911 he had a contract that provided that he be paid no salary, but would be given $10 once a week if he were sober. Even though he had worn out his welcome with Connie Mack and later with the St. Louis Browns, Rube created remarkably few, if any, problems for Joe Cantillon and the Millers.

During spring training in 1912 at Hickman, Kentucky, Waddell was one of the hardest workers in helping the residents try to save the local levee during a flood. And when the levee broke, Rube "did heroic service in helping the panic-stricken citizens to safety." It was also reported that while in Hickman, Rube spent many hours trying to train three wild geese to skip rope.

Waddell finished his career in 1913 with Virginia, Minnesota and Minneapolis in the Northern League. (Even though the records show that he pitched only for Virginia in 1913, he did appear in four games for Minneapolis's Northern League team earlier in the season, winning two, including a shutout.) By the time the season ended, Waddell had contracted tuberculosis. He returned to Minneapolis and continued to reside there until he left the next spring for a San Antonio sanitarium, where he died in April 1914. Waddell was elected to the Hall of Fame in 1946.

The Millers' drive for four pennants in a row was stopped by the Milwaukee Brewers on the final weekend of the 1913 season. That year there was baseball practically every day at Nicollet Park. The Northern League, a new Class-C organization, was formed and, with the permission of the local American Association teams, placed two of its clubs in Minneapolis and St. Paul. The experiment of maintaining teams in cities occupied by teams of superior classification proved unsuccessful. The St. Paul Northern League team was transferred to LaCrosse July 23. The Minneapolis entry, also owned by Mike Cantillon and known as both the "Roughriders" and "Little Millers," was more successful by reason of being in the race for first place all year, and it finished the season in Minneapolis.

Joe Cantillon remained with the Millers despite a strong lure from the Brooklyn entry in the newly-formed Federal League in 1914. Joe turned down an offer of a seven-year, $105,000 contract to manage the Brookfeds. The Millers rewarded his loyalty by winning another pennant in 1915. Mutt Williams led the Millers, and the American Association, with 29 wins and 441 innings pitched, and Earl Yingling captured the league ERA crown (the only Miller to ever do so), but it was a young lefthander who finished the season with a 5-9 record who copped the biggest headlines that season.

Harry Harper made his Miller debut May 11 with an 11-inning loss to Columbus despite striking out 16 batters. A week later Harry was on the short end of an 11-1 score as he walked 11 and struck out seven. After a rain out, Harper took the mound again and was a 4-0 winner over St. Paul, even though he walked 11 batters and hit two others. But he also struck out seven and held the Saints hitless. Two more days of rain put the wild southpaw on the mound for the third-straight game. Harper fanned ten but was a 5-1 loser to Indianapolis. After four games, Harry Harper had 45 strikeouts in 37 innings and a no-hitter, but only a 1-3 record to show for his work.

The pattern would continue. In the opener of the Independence Day doubleheader with the Saints, Harper went the distance in a 13-5 loss. Coming off a two-week layoff, Harry had apparently lost his fine edge; in only eight innings he walked 20 batters, setting a record unlikely to ever be broken. Two weeks later Harper was traded to the Washington Senators for right-hander Booth Hopper, who compiled a 19-3 record in the season's final two months.

Despite a horrendous start that found the team 12 games under .500 in June and in last place as late as July, the Millers rallied to edge out the Saints by a game-and-a-half for the league title.

The World War was by this time underway, but baseball paid no attention until just prior to the opening of the 1917 season when, on Good Friday, President Wilson signed a state-of-war resolution. George M. Cohan wrote a song for the occasion, the Doughboys started going "Over There," and Mike Cantillon responded in the proper spirit by having his Millers open their home season with new patriotic uniforms:

khaki color with red, white, and blue bands on the caps, belts, and hose, and a large American flag on the left breast.

Following the example of other teams, the Millers participated in military drills before games under the instruction of a non-commissioned officer. But while more than half of the players on the team's roster were eligible for the draft, the war had little impact on the Millers or baseball in 1917.

The year 1918 was a different story. With many potential fans fighting in Europe or working long hours in war-related industries; with the Millers losing many of their players to the service; and with the general uncertainty over the future of the game during the war, the Millers' Opening Day crowd was the smallest in their history. Drastic measures were needed to pull in fans, and on May 24 a season-high crowd of 1,200 showed up at Nicollet Park for the American Association's first-ever night game. There was no artificial lighting, but with the new Daylight Savings Time law in effect, a game in a northern city started at 7:00 p.m. could be completed under natural light. The new starting time was even responsible for a Miller win in June. Complaining of the lack of light, Columbus manager Joe Tinker pulled his team off the field prior to the start of a game, resulting in a 9-0 Miller forfeit victory.

Provost Marshal Enoch Crowder's "Work or Fight" order became effective July 1. Three weeks later Secretary of War Baker ruled that baseball was a "non-essential industry"; as a result, the American Association directors called an emergency meeting in Chicago, and, on July 21, the league brought its season to a premature close.

The end of the war in November meant the National Pastime would be back in business in 1919. For Dave Altizer, however, the news was of little consolation; the Miller shortstop's son had been killed in action in France less than a month before the armistice.

Almost obscured by the war clouds that season was news of the sale of the Millers by Mike Cantillon to a group of twenty-nine businessmen, headed by George Belden, president of the Minneapolis Athletic Club. Even though his brother was gone, Pongo Joe would stay at the helm for another five years.

There would be no more pennants waving at Nicollet Park during the Cantillon era, but there were a couple of second-place finishes, as well as some memorable plays and players. The 1920 season, though, belonged to the St. Paul Saints. After winning their first eight games, Mike Kelley's men finished the season with 115 wins, 28 and-a-half games ahead of the second-place Louisville Colonels.

The Millers of 1921 became the first Association team to top the century mark in home runs. Led by Dick Wade and ex-pitcher Reb Russell with 32 and 33, respectively, Minneapolis hit 120 home runs, breaking their own league record of 68, set in 1912. They also went the entire season without being shutout, that streak beginning in September 1920

and ending 238 games later in June 1922.

Also in 1921, Bill McKechnie finished his playing career at third base for Minneapolis. He had only a .234 lifetime average in the major leagues, but hit .321 for the Millers. Following his playing days, McKechnie compiled a long and successful record as a manager, winning pennants with three different National League teams (St. Louis, Pittsburgh and Cincinnati) and earning himself a spot in the Hall of Fame in 1961. (McKechnie had played for St. Paul in 1912 and is the only Hall of Famer to have played for both the Millers and the Saints.)

In 1922, the Millers' Morley Jennings became the only Association player ever to hit into an unassisted triple play – thanks to the slick fielding of Columbus shortstop Charley Pechous. Gavvy Cravath returned to Minneapolis that year and contributed four home runs as the team came within one of the home-run record they had set the previous year.

A 7-1 win against Indianapolis on October 7, 1923 closed the curtain on the Cantillon era. Following the season Joe Cantillon stepped down as field manager, and the twenty-nine owners sold out to a familiar figure. For the second time Mike Kelley would lead the team.

KELLEY—AGAIN

In 1924 Mike Kelley inherited a team whose better days were behind them, and so he began the job of rebuilding. Kelley is well remembered for for his "retooling factory"—buying aging major-leaguers, then selling them back to the majors after they had padded their averages in cozy Nicollet Park. But Mike proved to be a shrewd judge of young talent as well.

However, the reconstruction took time. One of the first deals Kelley made was a trade of outfielder Carl East, who had led the Association with 31 home runs in 1923, to the Washington Senators for outfielder George Fisher.

For the thirty-year-old East, the trade marked his return to the majors, with a team that would go on to win the World Series that year. East's previous big-league experience consisted of one pitching appearance with the St. Louis Browns in 1915.

But after only two games in Washington, East became angered over remarks made to him by Senators' owner Clark Griffith and left the club. Griffith then demanded the return of Fisher from Minneapolis. Over the protests of the Millers, Judge Landis, Commissioner of Baseball, ordered Fisher to report back to the Senators.

In early June, the Senators attempted to trade Fisher again, this time to the Milwaukee Brewers, bringing another strong reaction from Mike Kelley. This time, Judge Landis sided with Minneapolis and finally awarded Fisher to the Millers.

Happy to be in one place, Fisher hit .309 for the Millers but was unable to help them to anything better that a sixth-place finish in 1924.

In 1926, Kelley's men finished seventh, 32 1/2 games out of first (but still 32 games in front of last-place Columbus). As a result, Kelley seemed more interested in the performance of the Des Moines team, of which he was a half-owner, in the Western League. While in Louisville with the Millers late in the season, Kelley and coach Red Corriden went out to buy a western newspaper to check the progress of his other team. Crossing the street, Mike read the streamer, "Des Moines Clinches Pennant." His elation was brief, however; in the next instant Kelley was hit by a car, and suffered a badly broken left leg.

The breaks for Kelley and the Millers finally got better in 1928. Despite a slow start that season, the team caught fire, led by Duluth-native Spencer Harris. In his initial season with the Millers, Harris compiled a .327 average and led the Association in runs, doubles, total bases, home runs, and walks, while adding 127 RBI's (hitting mainly in the leadoff spot). During the ten years he would play with the Millers, Harris hit over .300 every year and six times topped the century mark in runs batted in. Speed and grace characterized his play in the pasture, making Harris the premier center fielder in the American Association in the 1930s.

Following his stay in Minneapolis, Spence played another ten seasons on the West Coast, finally ending a 28-year professional career at the age of 48. To this day, Harris remains the minor-league career leader in runs, hits, and doubles and is third on the all-time list with 3,258 games played.

That same year Zack Wheat finished his career in Minneapolis. Wheat had collected over 2,800 hits during 18 seasons with the Brooklyn Dodgers. He still had enough hits left to record a .309 average in 82 games for the Millers. Wheat was elected to the Hall of Fame in 1959.

The Millers were finally bumped from first place with a week left in the 1928 season and finished second, two-and-a-half games out.

The 1929 Millers won 33 of their first 46 games, but would crash harder than the stock market did later in the year, and finished the season 22 games behind the first-place Kansas City Blues. Still, it was a productive year for the team. But despite 20-victory seasons by John Brillheart and Rube Benton, Spencer Harris hitting .350, Wes Griffin playing all nine defensive positions in one game and the team setting a new league record with 158 home runs, the most memorable event of the 1929 season was "The Fight."

The donnybrook between the Millers and Saints in the morning game of the Fourth of July doubleheader at Nicollet Park was described by veteran baseball (and boxing) reporter George Barton as "the most vicious affair ever witnessed at Nicollet," which "required fully a dozen policemen to quell the disturbance."

The trouble began in the third inning when Hughie McMullen grounded to Saints' first-baseman Oscar Roettger. Pitcher Huck Betts covered first and was spiked by McMullen as he crossed the bag. The St. Paul and Minneapolis newspapers differed the next day as to whether the spiking was intentional, but apparently there was no doubt in Betts's mind as he took the ball from his glove and fired it at McMullen's head in retaliation. The throw missed but Sammy Bohne didn't. Bohne, the Millers' reserve infielder who was coaching first at the time, rushed Betts with a series of punches. The dugouts emptied and the fun was on. McMullen recalled that "Both clubs met in the pitcher's box, and you hit anyone near you." The headline over Halsey Hall's story in the *Minneapolis Journal* the next day read, "Sammy Bohne Doesn't Play, But Gets More Hits Than Those Who Do".

There were plenty of ejections in the game, but Hugh McMullen was not among the ejectees – ironic because in a letter written by McMullen fifty-five years later, Hughie admitted that he had indeed spiked Betts intentionally in retaliation for a bean-ball Betts had thrown a few pitches earlier.

Almost overlooked amid all the other 1929 happenings was the late-season purchase of slugger Nick Cullop from the Atlanta Crackers of the Southern Association.

For Cullop, the road to success in Minneapolis would be paved with adversity. During the off-season one of his children was killed after falling out a window of the family apartment in St. Louis. Two months later his other child died of a fever. At that time, his wife had a nervous breakdown and was ill for several months.

When the 1930 season finally began, Cullop was beaned in the team's third game, prompting a battle with ball shyness. In his next fifteen at-bats, Nick could muster only one hit while striking out eleven times. In the Millers' first 28 games, Cullop managed only one home run; but in the final 125 games he regained his confidence at the plate and finished the season with a league-record 54 home runs.

After a sixth-place finish by the Millers in 1931, Mike Kelley decided to leave the bench and confine his efforts to the front office. For the past two years he had delegated many of the field-manager duties to coach Bill Meyer; now, he found a full-time replacement in Donie Bush, the erstwhile pennant-winning

1931 Millers. *Minnesota Historical Society.*

manager of the 1927 Pittsburgh Pirates.

Donie's arsenal included holdovers Harris, short-stop Ernie Smith, and outfielders Art Ruble and Joe Mowry, and in the spring of 1932, the Millers acquired first-baseman Joe "Unser Choe" Hauser from the Baltimore Orioles of the International League.

Unser Choe (a German expression for "Our Joe") had received his nickname while playing for the Brewers in his hometown of Milwaukee in 1920. "Because I lived there, nobody was supposed to boo me," Joe explains, "but when I had a bad day and some fans did, others told them to knock it off because 'Das ist Unser Choe'."

Hauser came up to the majors with the Philadelphia Athletics in 1922 and had his best year two years later, at the age of twenty-five, when he hit .288 with 27 home runs and 115 RBI's. But a chance for an encore in 1925 was missed when he broke his leg in spring training and spent the entire season on the shelf. A comeback attempt in 1926 was hampered by his still-crippled leg, another season in the minors followed, but in 1928 he returned to the A's and appeared ready to resume what he had started in 1924. With six home runs and a .400-plus batting average during spring training, Hauser continued his torrid hitting through the first two months of the regular season; however, a sudden – and seemingly inexplicable – turnaround in his hitting ensued, and, one year later, he was back in the minors, this time to stay.

Hauser blames the premature end of his major-league career on a 1928 teammate with the Athletics – Ty Cobb. "Cobb had told me during spring training that he would help me with my hit-ting when we got north," Hauser recalled fifty-six years later. "About 35 to 40 games into the season, he started getting on me to crowd the plate. I had to nearly hit the ball with my elbows, and I could not hit like that."

In his 1960 autobiography, Ty Cobb remarked, "In all modesty, I could teach hitting." But one of his pupils, Joe Hauser, laments, "He drove me out of the big leagues by trying to teach me how to hit when I was already hitting .365."

Far away from Cobb, Hauser regained his batting touch with the Baltimore Orioles. He set an organized baseball single-season record with 63 home runs in 1930 and led the International League in homers again the following year before he was sold to the Millers just prior to the opening of the 1932 season.

The presence of Hauser prompted Mike Kelley to send the team's incumbent first baseman, George Kelly, the former New York Giant who would be elected to the Hall of Fame in 1973, to the Brooklyn Dodgers in exchange for Clyde "Pea Ridge" Day, the champion hog caller of Pea Ridge, Arkansas. Day had previously pitched for the Kansas City Blues and was well known within the American Association for his windmill windup, which he embellished with an ear-piercing hog call. A troubled man with a reputation for hard drinking, Day, two years later, would take his life by slicing his throat with a hunting knife.

Newcomers Andy Cohen at second and Foster "Babe" Ganzel at third would join Hauser and Ernie Smith to round out the infield of the Millers, who averaged nearly seven runs per game in 1932, setting a single-season record for runs scored that still stands.

Joe Mowry set an all-time Association record with 175 runs, Art Ruble led the league with a .376 average, and Hauser survived a slow start to take the Association home-run title with 49; Hauser missed a shot at Cullop's record when a bad knee sidelined him the final two weeks of the season.

The pitching staff was ancient but effective. Rosy Ryan topped Association hurlers with 22 victories, many in relief, while greybeards Jess Petty and Rube Benton combined for 34 wins between them.

The Millers won the pennant, their first since 1915, by nine-and-a-half games, and prepared for their first appearance in the Junior World Series, a post-season contest between the champions of the American Association and the International League, which had been held off and on since 1903.

Their opponents would be the Newark Bears, a powerful New York Yankees farm team that featured heavy-hitters Marv Owen, Red Rolfe, and Dixie Walker. Don Brennan, the "Merry Mortician," had led the International League with 29 wins.

Although the Millers could manage only 16 hits and five runs in the first three games of the series at Newark, they nevertheless captured two of those games behind fine mound performances by Petty and Frank "Dutch" Henry. Donie Bush was bursting with confidence on the train ride back to Minneapolis as he said, "As far as I'm concerned, the Little World Series will go to Minneapolis. I'm not boasting when I say this. The Bears will not win a game in our park."

But Don Brennan, who had shut the Millers out on four hits in Game One, won the fourth game, 5-2, to even the series at two games apiece.

Advertisement for 1932 Junior World Series. *Fred Souba.*

Game Five finally produced the slugfest most fans had expected. With the game tied, 8-8, the Bears had runners at first and third with two out in the ninth when Johnny Neun slashed a liner into left-center that centerfielder Harry Rice seemingly captured with a diving stab before sliding on the ground for a considerable distance. Both the second and third base umpires signalled out, ending the inning and bringing a group of charging Bears, led by manager Al Mamaux, out of the Newark dugout. After listening to their arguments, the umpires huddled and reversed their decision, saying that Rice had dropped the ball, which allowed the go-ahead run to score. Out came Donie Bush, demanding an explanation. Again, the arbiters called an impromptu conference, and, again, they came out with a different decision, ruling once again that Rice had caught the ball, which brought an encore performance by Mamaux. The scene continued – the men in blue listening to the remonstrations of the offended manager, huddling and emerging from their meeting with a decision opposite of their previous call – until a total of six decisions had been made and the game had been delayed more than forty minutes. Bush finally ended the rhubarb by lodging a formal protest of the game.

Unfortunately for Minneapolis, the committee that would rule on the protest was made up of an equal number of representatives of the American Association and International League. Thus the vote ended in a partisan deadlock; as a result, the Millers' protest was disallowed, and the Bears 12-9 victory was allowed to stand.

The next day a three-run, ninth-inning rally gave the game, 8-7, and the series, four games to two, to Newark.

Donie Bush's success with the Millers earned him another chance in the majors. Bush took the managerial job at Cincinnati in 1933, and Dave "Beauty" Bancroft, a former shortstop for the Phillies and Giants who would be elected to the Hall of Fame in 1971, was called in to fill his spot in Minneapolis.

Under Bancroft, the Millers finished second to Columbus, then lost to the Red Birds in a post-season series to determine who would advance to the Junior Series. Team accomplishments, however, were overshadowed by an individual performance.

Joe Hauser failed to homer in the team's first nine games of 1933. In the Millers' home opener, though, Unser Choe went the opposite way with a three-run homer over the left-field fence in his first at-bat of the season at Nicollet. Three more home runs, including a grand slam, followed the next day, and Joe was on a roll. His total by the end of June was 32, far in front of all rivals. Homers in seven-straight games in mid-July gave him 41, within striking distance of Nick Cullop's record with barely more than half the season gone. Hauser surpassed his previous year's output and reached the half-century mark in Milwaukee on July 27. Two weeks later he hit Number 55 in Toledo

to break Cullop's mark. He now held the single-season home run record in both the American Association and International League. A round-tripper on August 20 gave him the distinction of being the first (and still only) player to hit 60 home runs in a season twice. Now he set his sights on his own professional record of 63, which he had set three years earlier with the Orioles.

Hauser was stalled at 62 as the Millers went into the Labor Day doubleheader with the Saints. The new record did not appear likely to happen in the morning game at St. Paul. With a thirty-foot-high wall at the top of a ten-foot embankment, measuring 365 feet down the line, Lexington Park's right-field fence was the league's most uninviting target for southpaw swingers. Hitless in his first three at-bats in the game, Hauser responded with a drive over the distant wall in the seventh, then followed with anoth-

Photo sequence detailing the Play of Six Decisions. *Minneapolis Journal.*

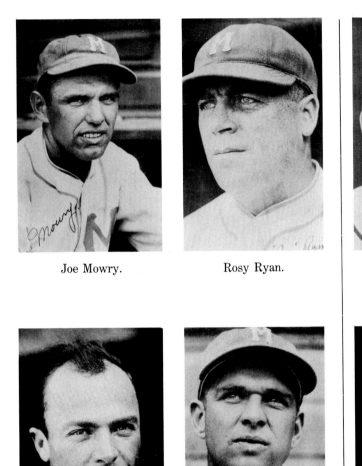

Joe Mowry.

Rosy Ryan.

Jess Petty.

Rube Benton.

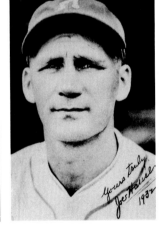

Spencer Harris.

Foster "Babe" Ganzel.

Joe Hauser.

Andy Cohen.

Members of the 1932 American Association Champions. *Fred Souba.*

er shot in the ninth to tie and break his own home-run record. In doing so, Joe also became the first player to hit two home runs in a game over Lexington's right-field fence since the park had been rebuilt in 1915. Hauser added five more home runs the following week, but his chance at 70 was washed out when rain cancelled the Millers' final game. Even so, at the Triple-A classification or higher level, Joe Hauser's benchmark of 69 home runs has never been duplicated.

Donie Bush returned to lead the Millers in 1934, and Hauser rolled off to his fastest start ever. With 17 home runs and 40 RBI's in the teams' first 20 games, Joe looked as though he would rewrite the record book again.

A knee injury in June sidelined Hauser for three weeks, but he picked up the pace upon his return to the lineup in July (even adding two home runs and six RBI's in the Association All-Star Game at Nicollet Park), and appeared certain to be the home-run king of his league for the fifth consecutive year. On July 29th, however, with 33 home runs already under his belt, Joe fractured his kneecap in Kansas City. Teammate Buzz Arlett, who hadn't even joined the Millers until late May, eventually passed the idle Hauser and took the league crown with 41 home runs.

Hauser was in a cast, but Ab Wright, in his first full season with the Millers, hit .353 with 29 home runs, while catcher Pinky Hargrave was named the league's Most Valuable Player. And with right-hander Wally Tauscher winning 21 games, the Millers were able to capture another pennant. Once again, however, a post-season series was held between the Millers and second-place Columbus to se-lect a representative for the Junior World Series. This time the runner-up Red Birds copped the series, sparking a storm of protest that resulted in the temporary abandonment of the post-season playoff system. Because of this, no Junior World Series was played in the following year.

But even without that as an incentive, in 1935 Donie Bush matched Joe Cantillon's earlier feat of winning the flag in his first three years with the team, as the Millers won another pennant, overcoming injuries at times so frequent that Kelley and Bush were on the verge of transporting their players from city to city in an ambulance.

In the second week of spring training Buzz Arlett suffered a torn ring finger on his left hand and part of the member had to be amputated. Babe Ganzel injured his eye running into a clothesline and later sprained an ankle getting off a train. Outfielder Dutch Holland was beaned in spring training and severely beaned again in June, suffering a broken jaw. Spencer Harris chipped a bone in his ankle, pitcher Ray Kolp wrenched a leg stepping in an outfield crevice and Wally Tauscher (who would still lead the team with 18 wins) was out for weeks with a sore shoulder. In addition, Pinky Hargrave twice suffered broken fingers and was shelved for the final two months of the season.

But among those who stayed healthy, rookie Johnny Gill led the Association with 43 home runs and 154 RBI's while hitting .361. Another newcomer, Fabian Gaffke, hit .302 with 19 home runs. A dangerous right-handed hitter, Gaffke was also an outstanding ball hawk in center field, and was considered to have one of the strongest throwing arms in the history of the Millers.

Russell "Buzz" Arlett

Born Oakland, Calif.,
Jan. 3, 1899

Nationality—German-English

Height 6' 2½", weight 218

Position—Outfield

Throws Right—Bats both ways

1st year
1918 Oakland P.C.L.

1919-30 incl., Oakland P.C.L.

1931 Philadelphia Nat. L.

1932 Baltimore Int. L.

1933 Baltimore Int. L.

Buzz Arlett. *Norwest Bank.*

Wally Tauscher. *Fred Souba.*

In 1936 the American Association adopted a playoff scheme called the "Governor's Cup," in which the top four teams from the regular season would battle for the title and a spot in the Junior Series. But despite being the first Association team to top 200 home runs in a season, the Millers could rise no higher than fifth place and missed the playoffs completely.

In 1938 Ted Williams made Minneapolis his final pit stop en route to Fenway Park and a Hall of Fame career with the Red Sox. As a nineteen-year-old in his second season of pro ball, Williams became the first player to win the American Association Triple Crown, hitting .366 with 43 home runs and 142 RBI's, leading the league in runs, total bases, and walks, as well. He was a unanimous selection as the starting

1935 MILLERS–AMERICAN ASSOCIATION CHAMPIONS
Bottom: Babe Ganzel; Fabian Gaffke; Leo Norris; Johnny Gill; Al Leitz; Doc Bowman, Trainer.
Middle: Shanty Hogan; Bill Perrin; Joe Hauser; Dutch Holland; Donie Bush, Mgr.; Mike Kelley; Andy Cohen; Spencer Harris.
Top: Rosy Ryan; Ray Kolp, Coach; Archie McKain; Denny Galehouse; Tony Wolcyn; Wally Tauscher; Buzz Arlett; Belve Bean; Buckshot May.

Ted Williams. *Minnesota Historical Society and Minneapolis Star and Tribune.*

right fielder in the Association All-Star Game in July.

With a temper as hot as his bat, Teddy Ballgame was nearly as famous for some of his outbursts as he was for his hitting. In a game against the Saints on August 9, after popping out on a pitch he thought he should have sent on a long journey across Nicollet Avenue, Williams returned to the dugout and smashed a water cooler with his fist, giving his teammates an early shower and nearly ending his career as a piece of glass barely missed a nerve in his hand. Legend has it that Ted's behavior reached the point where Donie Bush told Mike Kelley, "Either that kid goes or I go." Came the reply, "We're going to miss you, Donie."

After the Millers, Williams survived two wars to hit 521 home runs with the Red Sox, twice winning the American League Triple Crown and compiling a lifetime batting average of .344. His election to the Hall came in 1966.

Donie Bush resigned as skipper of the Millers after the 1938 season to take a similar post and become part-owner of the Louisville Colonels. Tom Sheehan, a former standout hurler who had won 31 games for the Saints in 1923, was brought in as the new manager.

Significant events of the 1939 season included Wally Tauscher's 100th win as a Miller, a new league record of 217 home runs by Minneapolis and 22 victories for Herb Hash as he led the league in that department and also became the Millers last 20-game winner.

A little man with a funny moustache was grabbing the world's largest headlines in 1940, but the biggest name in Minneapolis at that time was Ab Wright, a

Owners and managers of the Minneapolis Millers, 1902–1939. 1) Clarence
Saulpaugh. 2) Walter Wilmot. 3) Mike Cantillon. 4) Joe Cantillon. 5) George
Belden. 6) 1902 Millers. 7) Mike Kelley. 8) Donie Bush. 9) Dave Bancroft.
10) Tom Sheehan. *Minnesota Historical Society.*

Albert "Ab" Wright
Born Tulsa, Okla.,
Nov. 16, 1907
Nationality—Scotch-Irish
Height 6' 1¾", weight 185
Position—Outfield
Throws Right—Bats Right
1st year
1929 Bloomington 3 I. and
Joplin W.A. as pitcher
1930 Shawnee and Muskogee
A.A.
1931 Muskogee W.A. and
Minneapolis A.A.
1932 Minneapolis A.A.
Des Moines W.L.
Danville 3 I. L.
Greensboro
1933 Minneapolis A.A. and
Little Rock S.A.
Best year, 1931
Hit 377 to lead league

Ab Wright. *Norwest Bank.*

fixture in the Miller outfield and a right-handed hitter who thus did not enjoy the perquisites of Nicollet's short right-field line. Still, during his tenure with the Millers, which covered 892 games over all or part of ten different seasons, Abby hit .323 with 159 home runs.

In 1940 Wright exploded to win the Association Triple Crown with 39 home runs, 159 RBI's and a .369 average. His greatest fireworks came on the Fourth of July in the morning game against the Saints at Nicollet Park when he slugged four home runs and a triple for 19 total bases, still a league record.

Wright led the league in homers the following year, but was cost a shot at his third consecutive crown late in 1942 when he was skulled by a bottle thrown from the stands in Kansas City. The beaning also caused Wright to announce his retirement during the winter. The headaches and double vision cleared by the following May, however, and Wright rejoined the Millers, staying with them until he was sold to the Boston Braves in 1944.

By the early forties baseball and America braced themselves for another entrance into a world war. In June of 1941 Zeke Bonura, hitting .366 at the time, became the first Miller to leave for the Army. Minneapolis was still able to hold first place until August, thanks in large part to colorful newcomer Babe Barna.

Barna hit .336 with 24 home runs and led the league in stolen bases, a performance which earned Barna a trip to the majors with the New York Giants. Failing to make good in the big time, Babe returned to Minneapolis three years later and remained a Nicollet

Park favorite until 1948, as he twice led the league in home runs.

Barna had been a football, basketball and baseball standout at West Virginia University. Following his baseball career, Babe returned to his native state and operated a bar in Charleston. In May of 1972 he was inducted into the West Virginia Sports Hall of Fame. Seven days later, he died of a stroke.

The Millers wallowed in the second division during the final years of World War II. Baseball was allowed to continue operations during the war, although adjustments had to be made. As was the case during the First World War, the pool of available players, as well as fans, shrank considerably. Teams had to scramble to fill roster spots with players who were too young, too old, or physically unable to fight for Uncle Sam in Europe or the Pacific.

The curious collection of professional baseball talent during these years included a pitcher for the Cincinnati Reds who had yet to reach his sixteenth birthday (Joe Nuxhall) and an outfielder for the St. Louis Browns who had but one arm (Pete Gray).

Mike Kelley's answer to the manpower shortage was his "All-Nations" team in 1945. The Minneapolis roster included five Cubans, four of whom could not speak English, as well as American born athletes of Irish, Scandinavian, German, Polish, and Bohemian descent. Kelley tried to round out his aggregation by obtaining Cuban-Chinese infielder Manuel Hidalgo from Washington, but Senators' owner Clark Griffith was unwilling to part with him.

Meanwhile in Milwaukee, new Brewers' owner Bill Veeck was doing his part to provide entertainment to people working long hours in war-related jobs.

Babe Barna. *Shirley Crohn.*

47

The Brewers scheduled many morning games to accommodate the night shift, including a "Rosie the Riveter" game which started at 9:00 a.m. All women wearing welding caps or riveting masks were admitted free. The ushers, in nightgowns and nightcaps, served breakfast to the patrons.

Veeck also formed a band, of which he and manager Charlie Grimm (baseball's only left-handed banjo player) were a part. According to Veeck in his autobiography, the Brewer band had an excellent violin player, who was also a terrible pitcher. Veeck kept him on the roster the entire season just to play the violin, but rarely let him near the mound.

In addition to his banjo playing, Charlie Grimm could also do a hilarious Hitler imitation, which he performed for fans throughout the American Association.

With the end of the hostilities, Zeke Bonura, who had served in North Africa during the war, returned to the Millers as a player-manager in 1946. But Zeke was fired as manager and released as a player in early May.

Of greater significance was the sale of the Millers in April of that year by Mike Kelley to the New York Giants. For Kelley, it marked the end of a long association with our national pastime.

Born December 2, 1875 in Otter River, Massachusettes, his baseball prowess at Otter River High brought Kelley scholarship offers from Harvard, Dartmouth, Brown, and Amherst and pleas from his father to give up baseball and go into something "more stable." Instead, Mike signed a contract to play with Augusta, Maine in the New England League. Kelley later found himself at first base on a Louisville team that featured Honus Wagner, Rube Waddell, Fred Clarke, and Tommy Leach. His first appearance in the Twin Cities came when he joined the St. Paul team in the Western League in 1901, becoming its manager late in the season and staying with the Saints when they joined the American Association.

During his suspension that followed his 1906 Minneapolis debacle, Kelley managed in Des Moines and Toronto before his suspension was lifted and he returned to St. Paul in 1908. He managed the Saints, Indianapolis, and the Saints again until he bought the Millers in November of 1923. In all, Mike managed for thirty years in the minor leagues, winning 2,390 of 4,492 games.

Kelley held out as the last of the independent owners in the minor-leagues until he reluctantly consummated the deal with the Giants. Mike remained a year as honorary president of the club and lived in Minneapolis until his death in June of 1955.

With the end of Mike Kelley, it was also the end of home-owned minor-league baseball. Minneapolis would now join the rest of the minors in learning what it is like to be a farm team.

CORPORATE BASEBALL

The ramifications of changing from local ownership to being a farm club run by a group of moguls more than a thousand miles away took a while to sink in. In the early years of "corporate baseball" it still seemed to be business as usual for the Millers and their fans.

Before turning the team over to the Giants, Mike Kelley acted on one final brainstorm that produced a record crowd for Nicollet Park. Moving up a game with the Saints from later in the season to create a doubleheader in April of 1946, Kelley then ordered the ushers not to close the gates and to let all who desired to see the game in. The result was a paid attendance of 15,761, with 5,000 of those fans on the field, some within ten feet of the baselines. Special ground rules had to be implemented and all balls hit into the crowd were ruled doubles. The Millers and Saints ended up with 24 doubles in the twinbill as the Saints swept the doubleheader.

The Millers produced another Most Valuable Player in 1947 in reliever Steve Gerkin, who finished with a 10-2 record while appearing in 83 games.

The author of the league's top pitching feat that year, however, was Kansas City's Carl DeRose, a native of Milaca, Minnesota. DeRose had been out of action for three weeks with a "dead arm," and it was doubtful he would ever pitch again. Surgery on his arm was scheduled but he begged manager Bill Meyer for "one last chance" to pitch before the operation. On June 26 DeRose took the mound to face the Millers. From the third inning on, his arm hurt so bad that tears streamed down his face as he threw, but he continually refused Meyer's offer to lift him. And when pinch-hitter Babe Barna looked at a called third strike on a 3-2 count to end the game, Carl DeRose had completed the first perfect game in the history of the American Association. In the locker room after the game, DeRose was unable to even lift

Billy Herman. *Shirley Crohn.*

his arm far enough to shake hands.

In 1948 manager Frank Shellenback resigned abruptly when he became ill and was advised by doctors to take the rest of the year off. Centerfielder Frank "Chick" Genovese assumed the duties on an interim basis, and in mid-June the Millers hired Billy Herman to manage the team the remainder of the season. Herman also played in ten games near the end of the season, hitting .452 with two home runs.

Herman had hit .304 in 15 seasons in the majors and had been named to the National League All-Star

team ten straight years before coming to the Millers. He would be inducted into the Hall of Fame in 1975.

Integration came to the Association on May 22, 1948 when Roy Campanella appeared behind the plate for the St. Paul Saints, who were by this time a Brooklyn Dodger farm team. The first blacks in Miller uniforms would appear a year later when General Manager Rosy Ryan signed Ray Dandridge and Dave Barnhill off the roster of the New York Cubans of the Negro American League; the pair made their debut for the Millers in June of 1949.

Ray Dandridge, a sixteen-year veteran of the Negro and Mexican Leagues, was regarded as the greatest third baseman in the history of the Negro Leagues. With the Newark Eagles in the late 1930's, Dandridge was a member of the "Million-Dollar Infield," so called because it was said that's what it would have been worth had the players been white.

In the early forties, Dandridge left Newark to play in the Mexican League. He became a close friend and a trusted confidant of league president Jorge Pasquel, who often sent Ray back to the states to recruit other Negro League players.

At one point Dandridge and Pasquel had a falling out after a salary dispute. Dandridge was on his way back to the United States when his train was stopped by the Mexican Army, who informed Dandy that Pasquel had changed his mind and was prepared to raise his salary.

Despite the occasional hard feelings between the two, Dandridge remained loyal to Pasquel, and even turned down an offer by Bill Veeck to play with the Cleveland Indians in 1947. In 1948, though, Dandridge returned north and became the player-manager for the New York Cubans until he and

Ray Dandridge applies tag to St. Paul's Gino Cimoli. *Minneapolis Star and Tribune.*

Barnhill left to join Minneapolis.

Dandridge was thirty-five at the time, but claimed he was only thirty. (After the color line had been broken, many older Negro Leaguers shaved a few years off their age, hoping for an opportunity to play in the majors.) For Dandridge, however, that chance did not come.

Besides his age, there are other explanations as to why he was never called up by the New York Giants. The Giants already had three blacks on their roster, and an informal quota system was said to still exist. In addition, Giants president Horace Stoneham told Dandridge he was too good a drawing card in Minneapolis to be moved to New York. There was even speculation that his chances were hurt because of his involvement in the Mexican League, which, by the late forties, was viewed as an "outlaw league" when it began raiding players from the American and National League rosters. Although never given the chance to play in the majors, Dandridge was elected to the Hall of Fame in 1987.

In his rookie season at Minneapolis Dandridge hit .311 and had a 28-game hitting streak during the year. He also had three home runs and eight RBI's in one game in August.

Dandridge helped the Millers in 1949 to top the 200 mark in homers for the third time in their history (they were the only Association team ever to reach that level), with Charlie Workman of Minneapolis leading the league with 41 home runs. The Millers finished in fourth place, qualifying for the playoffs. Since the four-team playoff series had begun in 1936, the Millers had been unable to ever advance beyond the first round. Their fourth-place finish in 1949 would only earn them another case of snakebite.

In their opening playoff series with Indianapolis, Minneapolis won the first three games—all on the road. Coming home needing only one win at Nicollet Park to break their playoff jinx, the Millers dropped Game Four, 16-2. Prospects were still bright, however; Jack Harshman, who had finished second to Workman with 40 home runs during the regular season, had homered in each of the first four playoff games. But Harshman's halo would turn to goat horns in the fifth game.

Up by a run in Game Five, the Millers were on the verge of breaking the game open with the bases loaded and two out in the sixth. Dave Barnhill drilled a liner to left for an apparent triple and three runs. But Harshman, who had been on second, was called out on appeal for missing third. With the final out of the inning coming on a force out, all runs on the play were erased, leaving the door open for an Indian comeback. Indianapolis won the game, 9-8, then captured the final two games to win the series and continue the legacy of post-season frustration for the Millers.

Halsey Hall rated the Millers a "darkhorse" in 1950, but Ray Dandridge's performance in the field and at the plate (a .311 batting average with 106 runs scored and 80 batted in), earned him the league's Most Valuable Player award. Teammate Bert Haas finished second in the balloting.

The Miller lumber company that year tied a league record by scoring 28 runs in a game against the Saints on Memorial Day. (Haas later recalled second-year manager Tommy Heath's fidgeting during a ninth-inning St. Paul rally in that game. According to Haas, Heath continued hustling pitchers to the bullpen as the Saints cut the Miller lead to 19.)

On the pitching side for the Millers in 1950, Dixie

Howell twirled a no-hitter en route to a 14-2 season, and Hoyt Wilhelm, working primarily as a starting pitcher, posted a 15-11 mark. Wilhelm won 11 more games for the Millers the following year and Tommy Heath said, "I'd like to see Wilhelm get something to go along with his knuckleball."

But with little more than a knuckler, Wilhelm embarked on a major-league career that would last 21 seasons and include more than 1,000 appearances on the mound. He was elected to the Hall of Fame in 1985.

Hoyt Wilhelm. *Shirley Crohn.*

When the 1950 season closed the Millers had grabbed their eighth Association pennant, but would encounter a too-familiar scene in the playoffs as, once again, they were eliminated in the opening round.

The Millers were picked to repeat as pennant winners in 1951, largely because of a new center fielder who, it was assumed, would spend the entire season in Minneapolis before graduating to the majors. But the New York Giants decided they needed Willie Mays sooner than that, and, in May, Minneapolis saw its new hero disappear before most fans even had a chance to see him play.

His statistics with the Millers make it obvious why the Giants couldn't wait: a .477 average, eight home runs, 30 RBI's and 38 runs scored in 35 games. Mays nearly single-handedly carried the Millers through the first month of the season as the Millers won 21 of those games.

He was equally awesome roaming center field. In early May at Nicollet Park, Louisville's Taft Wright drilled a liner to right-center. Somehow Willie got to it, leaping against the wall and snagging the ball before it hit the fence. Meanwhile, Wright put his head down and hustled into second base, assuming he had a stand-up double and was incredulous when the umpire informed him he was out. Wright remained at second until manager Pinky Higgins came out and told him that Willie indeed had caught the ball.

After leaving Minneapolis, Mays became the National League's Rookie of the Year and helped lead the Giants to the 1951 pennant. Following his career with the Giants and Mets, which ended in 1973, Mays was elected to the Hall of Fame in his first year of eligibility in 1979.

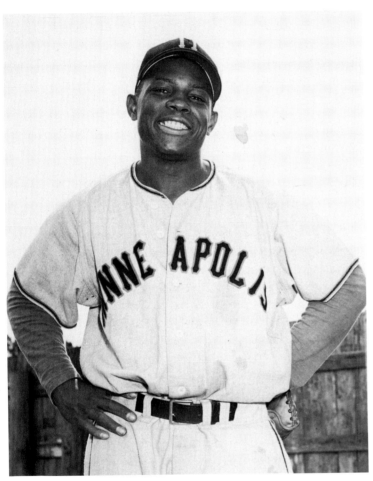

Willie Mays. *Shirley Crohn.*

Willie Mays (right) at spring training with Millers in 1951. *Minneapolis Star and Tribune.*

Mays wasn't the first, but to that point he was the most significant, player to be plucked in mid-season by the parent Giants. Recalls of other Miller players followed, prompting *Minneapolis Tribune* columnist Dick Cullum to claim, "Baseball on the Triple-A farm is mere exhibition training and is not being conducted with an earnest effort to win games." On the same subject, Halsey Hall remarked, "Let Rosy Ryan and Tommy Heath have the gold removed from their teeth and send it to the New York (Giants) front office. They'll get it sooner or later anyway."

The A. M. (After Mays) Millers were also upstaged by the prospects of the area getting its own major-league team. The first geographic shuffling of major-league teams in half a century had brought big-league status to Milwaukee; Twin Citians hoped they would not be far behind.

A task force was formed for the purpose of luring a team to Minneapolis. The early consensus of the group was that, to accomplish their goal, a new stadium was necessary. A diamond at Parade Stadium was looked at as a possible residence until a new park could be erected, but the task force decided to concentrate on first building a new stadium.

(A few years earlier the Minneapolis Baseball Association had acquired thirty-three acres of land on Wayzata Boulevard, a quarter-mile west of the Belt Line, and preliminary architectural work had been started on construction of a stadium for the site. But with the outbreak of the Korean War came a government ban on construction of new sports arenas, and the land remained dormant.)

In early 1955 a bond drive was led by local business interests known as the Minneapolis Minutemen to finance construction of another stadium, and on June 20, 1955 ground was broken on a cornfield in suburban Bloomington. St. Paul was noticeably absent in its support of the project, and St. Paul Mayor Joseph Dillon said "under no circumstances" would his city support a Bloomington site. Instead, St. Paul began construction of its own stadium in the Midway area of St. Paul. With Walter O'Malley of the Brooklyn Dodgers on hand, St. Paul held its ground-breaking ceremonies two weeks prior to that done in Bloomington.

The battle of the stadiums would also mean new playpens for the Millers and Saints and signal the mortality of the stately Nicollet and Lexington structures.

The Millers opened their 1955 season aware that this would be their last year in Nicollet Park. Their fortunes for the season would ride, as usual, on their hitting, which was led by George Wilson, who, in 1953, had won the league home-run crown despite missing the Millers' first 36 games, and Bob Lennon, who had hit 64 home runs for Nashville of the Southern Association in 1954.

Al Worthington was the staff's pitching ace. Worthington had started the season with the Millers the previous two years, but had been called up in midseason by the Giants each year. (In 1953 he pitched a shutout in his first two major-league outings.) Worthington would lead the Association in 1955 with 19 wins, but the Miller mound help thinned out quickly from there. Al's 3.58 earned-run-average was the lowest on the team. Jim Constable, with the team's second-best ERA, gave up nearly a run per game more.

55

A ball signed by the 1955 champion Millers is dropped into concrete being poured for Met Stadium, September 1955. *Minneapolis Star and Tribune.*

Left: Lexington Park, home of the St. Paul Saints. *Minnesota Historical Society and St. Paul Pioneer Press.*

Under second-year skipper Bill Rigney, Minneapolis got off to a fast start in 1955. In June the New York Giants came to Nicollet Park for an exhibition game. Despite a long home run by Willie Mays off Ralph Branca, the Millers won the game, 9-5. When the Giants left town after the game, they took with them Minneapolis second baseman Wayne Terwilliger and left behind outfielder Monte Irvin for the Millers.

Irvin was a veteran of the Negro Leagues (he was a teammate of Ray Dandridge's with Newark in 1938) and had been considered by many as the best choice to be the player to break major-league baseball's color barrier. Jackie Robinson would instead become the first black in organized baseball in the twentieth century, but Irvin got his chance with the Giants in 1949.

Bill Rigney had been a teammate of Irvin's on the Giants in 1951, and recalled that it was Monte who carried the team during a 16-game winning streak that helped the Giants overcome a 13 1/2 game deficit and eventually overtake Brooklyn for the pennant.

Irvin would have a similar hot streak for the Millers during a winning streak later in the year, and Monte hit .352 with 14 home runs in his half-season with Minneapolis. He returned to the majors and completed his playing career with the Chicago Cubs the next year and was voted into the Hall of Fame by the Negro League Committee in 1973.

The Millers held first place in mid-July; as a result, they earned the right to host their fourth Association All-Star Game, but a slump that followed dropped the team into third place in August. On August 4, though, Worthington won his 14th game to start a 15-game Minneapolis winning streak that shot the Millers back into first and left all other contenders far behind.

57

They won the pennant by nine games. Lennon, despite missing a month of the season with a bad shoulder, shared the team lead, with Wilson, in home runs with 31, and the Millers set a new league record with 241 homers. Third baseman Rance Pless led the league in batting average and was named the Association's Most Valuable Player.

Rance Pless forcing out Kansas City's Marv Throneberry at third. *Minneapolis Star and Tribune.*

The Millers celebrated their ninth pennant and prepared for the opening playoff round with the Denver Bears, a Yankee farm club managed by Ralph Houk. With a roster that included Marv Throneberry, who had led the league in home runs and RBIs, Bobby Richardson, Whitey Herzog, Woody Held, and Ralph Terry.

Denver held an 8-5 lead going into the last of the ninth in the first game of the series at Nicollet Park. But back-to-back home runs by Don Bollweg and Wilson (his third of the game) cut the lead to one. A double by Irvin and bunt single by Pless put the tying run at third. Irvin had to stay put as Lennon popped out and Joe Brachitta fanned, but Eddie Bressoud singled to tie the game and put the winning run in scoring position. Dave Garcia then blooped a single into short left. Pless and the throw arrived at the plate at the same time, but Pless won the collision with catcher Darrell Johnson as he knocked the ball loose and scored the winning ran.

The Millers had hit five home runs in the first game, and the next night they added three more as they took a two-game lead in the series.

In Game Three in Denver, the Millers grabbed a 5-0 lead, then held on for a 9-7 victory and were within one win of their first-ever playoff series victory. However, it appeared the series would be prolonged as the Bears carried a 6-3 lead into the ninth inning of the fourth game. But Monte Irvin still remembers the announcement that came over the public-address system at that time, which seemed to wake the Millers up: "Tomorrow's game will start at 6:00. Come early because we expect a sellout." "This game isn't over yet," growled George Wilson. George then hit a grand-slam and Irvin followed with a solo shot to give the Millers an 8-6 lead. But Whitey Herzog's two-run single in the last of the ninth kept the Bears alive. Finally in the 13th, Rance Pless homered to give the game and the series to the Millers. Minneapolis had hit 14 home runs in the series and Worthington had pitched in all four games without a decision.

The Millers would now face the Omaha Cardinals in the league championship for the right to advance to the Junior Series.

Minneapolis took the first two games, both slugfests at Nicollet, but encountered a pitching duel in Game Three in Omaha. With the game scoreless after six, Omaha's Stu Miller was working on a no-hitter as he faced Irvin to open the seventh. On an 0-1 pitch, Irvin checked his swing and the pitch was called a ball by plate-umpire Eddie Taylor. Rance Pless, who was on deck, later recalled that Miller "had taken something off his change up and Monte had a full swing before the ball was halfway to the plate." Taylor, though, not only stuck to his decision, but ejected Stu Miller for arguing the call. Cardinal fans, seeing their pitcher thrown out while working on a no-hitter, began hurling seat cushions and other debris onto the field. To restore order, league president Ed Doherty, who was in the box seats, overruled Taylor and allowed Miller to stay in the game, bringing Bill Rigney out of the Minneapolis dugout to lodge a protest.

When the game resumed Miller retired Irvin and Pless, but lost his no-hitter and shutout when Lennon sent a towering fly over the 380-foot mark in left-center.

Whitey Konikowski was working on a two-hitter for the Millers until he gave up two home runs in the eighth that gave Omaha a 3-1 win.

With Minneapolis's protest still pending, President Doherty called the opposing managers and the four umpires together for a midnight meeting at a downtown hotel, at which time Doherty overturned his own earlier decision to allow Stu Miller to stay in the game, ordering the game replayed from the point of protest, with Miller ejected from the game. Ironically, this meant Miller's no-hitter was once again intact, although he would not be allowed the chance to complete it.

When the protested game resumed the next afternoon, Bob Tiefenauer took Stu Miller's place on the mound and got Irvin to ground his first pitch to shortstop Dick Schofield, who booted it for an error. Pless followed with a sacrifice to bring up Lennon, whose home run the night before had been Minneapolis' first hit. This time he tripled high off the center-field fence, narrowly missing another home run, to score Irvin and give himself the possible distinction of being the first player ever to break up a no-hitter twice in the same game. Lennon was squeezed home by Dave Garcia, and the Millers added five in the eighth en route to a 7-2 win. They took the regularly scheduled game as well, to sweep the series and move onto the Junior World Series for the first time since their 1932 fiasco with Newark.

Aided by Doherty's ruling on the protest, the Millers became the first team in American Association history to win eight-straight playoff games. They made it nine in a row with an opening victory in the Junior Series versus the International League champion Rochester Red Wings.

The Red Wings won three of the next four games for a three-game-to-two lead and carried a 3-2 lead into the last of the eighth inning in Game Six. But George Wilson, who was 0-for-16 in the series coming into the game, homered to tie the score. In the tenth, Wilson drove another one onto Nicollet Avenue to win the game and knot the series at three games apiece. Al Worthington worked the final three innings to earn his third win of the series.

A sellout crowd was on hand the evening of September 28 to witness both the outcome of the Junior Series and the final game ever played at Nicollet Park.

Short on fresh arms, Rigney called on his bullpen ace, Bud Byerly, to start his first game of the season. He didn't last long. Howie Phillips greeted Byerly with a lead-off home run. The Wings added another run, and Bud gave way to Floyd Melliere after only

The 1955 Junior World Series Champions. *Pete Chubb.*

2/3 of an inning.

The 2-0 Rochester lead held until the fourth when a two-out Miller rally was capped by Lennon's three-run homer. Carl Sawatski followed with another home run, and Irvin made it 5-2 with a solo shot in the sixth.

When the Red Wings scored two runs in the seventh the call went to the bullpen for a weary Worthington, who trudged in and put out the fire. The Millers then gave Al some breathing room with four runs in their half of the seventh.

Worthington fanned the first two Red Wing bat-

Clubhouse celebration following the Millers' victory in the 1955 Junior World Series. *Minneapolis Star and Tribune.*

The Millers line up before the first game at Met Stadium, April 24, 1956. *Minneapolis Star and Tribune.*

ters in the ninth, then gave up a pair of base hits. But Jackie Brandt tried to bunt for a hit and Worthington threw him out at first to give the Millers their first Junior World Series championship and Nicollet Park a fitting farewell.

The parent club rewarded Bill Rigney's performance by promoting him to manager of the New York Giants, and Eddie Stanky was at the helm when the Millers opened their 1956 season in the new Bloomington ball park, which would eventually be called Metropolitan Stadium.

One of the most memorable incidents in the sixty-year history of Nicollet Park was the "Play of Six Decisions" in the 1932 Junior World Series. But the 18,366 fans who turned out to the Millers' new home got to see a "Play of Four Decisions" in the stadium's first game.

In the fifth inning of that game, the Wichita Braves' Joe Koppe tried to steal home, but was called out at the plate by umpire Bob Phillips. Braves' manager George Selkirk argued that catcher Vern Rapp had dropped the ball. Phillips thought he was protesting that a balk had been committed and called the runner safe. After a beef from Millers' skipper Stanky, Phillips checked with the third-base umpire, who said there had been no balk. Phillips then reversed his call to 'out' again. Selkirk charged back out of the dugout, screaming, "I didn't say he balked. I said he (the catcher) dropped the ball." Once again, Phillips conferred with the third-base umpire and, after being informed that Rapp had indeed dropped the ball, ruled the runner safe.

At that point, Stanky drop-kicked his hat and, along with Rapp, was kicked out of the game.

Rapp's replacement, Jake Jenkins, hit the first

Manager Eddie Stanky, about to be ejected from the first game at the new stadium. *Minneapolis Star and Tribune.*

63

home run in the new stadium in the sixth inning, but the Braves came back with two runs in the eighth to win the game, 5-3.

Later that season, Minneapolis fans witnessed a record-breaking performance as part of a pregame exhibition. Millers' outfielder Don Grate heaved a baseball from beyond the center-field fence toward home plate a distance of 445 feet-one inch, bettering by nearly two feet his own world record, which he had set in 1953. (Grate's record was broken by nine inches less that a year later by Glen Gorbous of the Omaha Cardinals.)

The opening of the new park renewed hopes of a major-league team coming to the area. Rumors of a possible Giants move to Minneapolis had been in the air and picked up intensity when Giants' president Horace Stoneham said, "This is definitely our last year in New York." It was also revealed that Stoneham had been engaged in negotiations with the Minneapolis major-league task force. But hopes were squashed when Stoneham instead moved the Giants to San Francisco following the 1957 season.

With that move also came the transfer of the Minneapolis Millers to Phoenix. To fill the vacancy, the San Francisco Seals, a Boston Red Sox farm club, were moved to Minneapolis.

The new Millers hired Gene Mauch to manage the team and play second base. Mauch's coaching staff included Hall of Famer Jimmie Foxx.

The Millers finished third in 1958, but beat Wichita

Gene Mauch (right), who played for and managed the Millers in 1958 and 1959. *Minneapolis Star and Tribune.*

and Denver in the American Association playoffs and then swept the Montreal Royals in four games to win their second Junior Series championship. Again in 1959, the Millers could finish no better than second, but made the most of their opportunity in the post-season playoffs.

The opening playoff round with Omaha was tied at two games each. In Game Five on September 15 at Metropolitan Stadium, a new second baseman, activated by the Millers just before game time, hustled home with the winning run in the last of the tenth.

Afterward, Omaha General Manager Bill Bergesch announced he was protesting the game, challenging the eligibility of the new second baseman. Ruling that the player had not been certified to play until September 18, league president Doherty upheld the protest and ordered the game replayed.

The next night the Millers won the replayed game, as well as the regularly scheduled contest, to capture the league semi-final series without the services of their new second baseman, Carl Yastrzemski.

With Yaz officially eligible, the Millers defeated the Fort Worth Cats for the league championship and a berth in the Junior World Series against the Havana Sugar Kings.

From every angle, the Havana-Minneapolis series was the most fantastic and colorful of all the Junior Series. Not only did it produce the highest receipts and second-largest attendance in history, but it was the only Junior World Series in which the submachine guns outnumbered the bats. Former pitcher Fidel Castro and his bearded troopers were on hand for each game played in Havana.

The first three games of the series were scheduled for Minneapolis, but cold weather virtually froze out the Millers end of the set. Attendance was sparse at the first two games as the Sugar Kings, unaccustomed to the climate, huddled around a fire in a wastebasket in their dugout to stay warm. When the cold postponed the third game, the Junior Series Commission shifted the remaining games to the Cuban capital.

The five games played in Havana attracted over 100,000 fans, not to mention several thousand of Castro's soldiers, who got in free, stationing themselves in the dugouts and lining the field with their bayonets exposed.

Minneapolis battled back from a three-game-to-one deficit to capture the fifth and sixth games, and they carried a 2-0 lead into the eighth inning of Game Seven. But the Kings rallied for two in the eighth to tie the game and won it on Don Morejon's run-scoring single in the last of the ninth.

But Millers pitcher Ted Bowsfield recalled twenty-five years later, "Nobody minded losing the game in that country and under those conditions. We were just happy to get out of town with our hides. During every game we could hear shots being fired, and we never knew what was going on."

Lefty Locklin remembered warming up before the seventh game when Castro made his entrance, passed the Minneapolis players in the bullpen, put his hand on his revolver and said, "Tonight we win."

The Millers had a new manager in 1960 as Mauch was abruptly summoned to Philadelphia to become manager of the Phillies. Eddie Popowski directed the Minneapolis in what would be its final season, and the Millers had one final star to showcase.

Carl Yastrzemski steals second. *Minneapolis Star and Tribune.*

Like Ted Williams twenty-two years earlier, Carl Yastrzemski would spend a season tuning up with the Millers before heading for a long in Boston, where, ironically, he would succeed Williams in left field.

After signing a professional contract following his freshman year at Notre Dame University, Yaz had won the batting crown in the Carolina League in 1959 before joining the Millers for their post-season playoffs in the fall. Carl hit.277 with one home run in the Junior World Series against Havana.

The Millers finished fifth in 1960, missing the playoffs, but for Yastrzemski, the man who was "as tough to get out as his name is to pronounce," the season was a success. He had a 30-game hitting streak during the year, hitting .432 during that stretch and hoisting his season average 23 percentage points to take over the league lead in that department. Yaz was eventually edged out by Denver's Larry Osborne for the batting title, but still wound up with a .339 average.

Yastrzemski would go on to play twenty-three years for the Boston Red Sox, winning the Triple Crown in 1967, and retiring with more than 400 home runs and over 3,000 hits. He was elected to the Hall of Fame in 1989.

The Millers played their final game September 11, beating Houston, 5-2, and finished the season with an 82-72 record.

By this time a major-league team for the area seemed inevitable. In 1959 the Continental League was formed, malting a bid to become a third major league. Minneapolis-St. Paul was to be one of the five founding members who would make up the eight-team league.

But on October 27, 1960 at 2:15 p.m. American League president Joe Cronin announced, "The present Washington club, will be moved to Minneapolis-St. Paul next year and will play its games in Metropolitan Stadium."

It had taken three attempts by Washington Senators president Calvin Griffith to get the permission of his fellow magnates to move to Minnesota, and it ended seven years of strenuous efforts by local interests to land a team.

However, major-league status for Minnesota would also mean the end of the Millers and Saints. When the two teams packed up their spikes and shin guards for the final time, they had left a legacy of winning baseball for the incoming Twins to follow.

In their fifty-nine years in the league the Millers had won 4,800 games and lost 4,366 for a.524 winning percentage, best by far of all the teams who had ever played in the American Association. The Saints had the second-best record. The Millers and Saints also shared the league record for pennants won, with nine each.

In addition, Minneapolis earned the right to host the Association All-Star game five times, more than any other city. And the Millers held the distinction of being the only Association team never to finish in the cellar.

But Twin Citians were too busy celebrating the. coming of major-league baseball to notice the loss of the Millers and Saints.

The state, as well as the rest of the region, was eager to say hello to the Minnesota Twins. There was no one left to say good bye.

Nicollet Park's right-field fence, 1939. *Minnesota Historical Society and Minneapolis Star-Journal.*

EPILOGUE: NICOLLET PARK

The Minneapolis Millers had a number of locales to hang their hats during their nearly eighty years of professional baseball: the original park at the corner of Chicago Avenue and 17th Street, in the days when handlebar mustaches were in vogue; another in the vicinity of the Milwaukee railroad shops bounded by 28th and 30th Streets and 24th and 26th Avenues in south Minneapolis; the band box in back of the West Hotel downtown; Minnehaha Driving Park and a field in White Bear Lake for Sunday games; and eventually Metropolitan Stadium, south of the city limits. But the park most closely associated with the Millers was the one described by former *Minneapolis Tribune* writer Dave Mona as "soggy, foul, rotten and thoroughly wonderful Nicollet Park".

Built at a cost of $4,000 to seat 4,000 fans, Nicollet Park, in its first season as well as its last, was home to a pennant winner. Also a center for prize fights and high-school football games, Nicollet is best remembered for its short right-field fence, only 279 feet, 10 inches from home plate.

Mike Kelley built his 1930s powerhouse around that fence, pouncing on sinewy southpaw swingers who could bombard Nicollet Avenue beyond. Halsey Hall remembers the right-field fence being made a little higher over the years—and awnings going down in front of the plate-glass windows on Nicollet Avenue businesses as insurance rates on window breakage rose.

The constant possibility of late-inning rallies kept fans in their seats until the very end. A typical Nicollet finish occurred in 1953 in the afternoon game of the Independence Day doubleheader. Trailing the Saints, 9-8, the Millers had two out and nobody on in the ninth when Clint Hartung walked and Ray Katt lifted a pop fly toward right that was caught by the breeze. When the ball came down it scraped the screen under the grandstand roof for a game-winning home run.

Sunday doubleheaders were often cut short by a law requiring games to be stopped promptly at 6:00 p.m. (The ordinance was repealed in 1941, but Mike Kelley continued to honor the policy.) In 1935 the

Millers saw a 3-0 lead disappear as Toledo scored five runs in the top of the ninth. But the clock at Nicollet read 5:54 as the Millers came to bat. With shrewd stalling by Fabian Gaffke, Buzz Arlett and Joe Hauser, the clock struck six o'clock before the final out was made; as a result, the score reverted back to the last full inning, wiping out the Mud Hen runs and giving the Millers a 3-0 win.

That same season Babe Ruth made a Nicollet Park appearance in a game between the Minneapolis and St. Paul police teams. Ruth played half a game with each team, and contributed a double in five trips to the plate. Pitching for the Minneapolis Police team, Pete Guzy, former East High and Minnesota Gopher pitching sensation and later the longtime football and baseball coach at Edison High, was able to count Babe as one of his 18 strikeout victims in the game.

Opposing right fielders at Nicollet remember Mike Kelley's Dalmatians—which were kept in the right-field corner in the field of play and would growl threateningly at any player in a visitor's uniform having to chase a batted ball into that area.

And it was the walls of Nicollet Park that Wheaties used to first unveil its "Breakfast of Champions" slogan in 1933.

The holiday doubleheaders at Nicollet and Lexington Parks—a morning game in one park and a seven-mile streetcar ride across the river for the afternoon game in the other—were the high points of the season for Millers and Saints fans.

In 1983 a historical marker was erected in front of the Norwest Bank on 31st and Nicollet, on the former site of Nicollet Park. The plaque was paid for in large part by donations from ex-players and fans. With their contributions came letters and notes to indicate that memories of Nicollet Park have not faded.

"Nicollet Park holds the best memories in baseball for me," says Al Worthington. The hero of the 1955 playoffs recalls that he had great success at Nicollet Park (his three-year won-loss record at Nicollet was 24-5). Al also remembers the lack of heat in the clubhouse. "It was so cold in April that taking a shower was almost like being outside when the sub-zero wind blew."

Hughie McMullen, who played in the late twenties, remembers even then Nicollet as a very old, run down park. "The fences were held up only by the paint on them", says McMullen.

Eddie Popowski managed the Millers in their final year at Met Stadium. But as an outfielder with Louisville in 1943, he played at Nicollet and recalls players having their gloves and shoes chewed up by rats when they left them overnight.

Professional baseball fans in the Upper Midwest can now watch baseball without real grass, sun, or rain. But for sixty years the small, wooden structure at the corner of 31st and Nicollet was home to ten pennant-winning teams, and was the mecca for thousands of baseball fans.

NICOLLET
BASEBALL PARK

— ■ ● ● ● ■ —

For 60 years -- 1896 through 1955 -- Nicollet Park, located in this block, rang with the cheers of Minneapolis Miller baseball fans. Spectators came from all across the upper midwest to watch the best baseball in the region. On one occasion it was reported that the entire town of Buhl, Minnesota -- 530 people -- motored down to the city to watch the Millers play. The park drew its largest crowd ever on April 29, 1946, when 15,761 people watched a double header between the Millers and the St. Paul Saints. The seating capacity of the park was 8,500. The Saints won both games.

Many of baseball's big names played and managed at Nicollet Park, some for the Millers and some as visitors. Among them were Ted Williams, Hobe Ferris, Perry Werden, Mike and Joe Cantillon, Joe Hauser, Gene Mauch, Hoyt Wilhelm, Rube Waddell, Rosy Ryan, Bill Rigney, Herb Score, Al Worthington, Donie Bush, Mike Kelley, Spencer Harris, Ray Dandridge, and Willie Mays.

In 1983 a plaque was erected to mark the site of Nicollet Park. *John Gaterud, Minnesota Times.*

Clint Hartung, the "Hondo Hurricane" slides into second. *Minneapolis Star and Tribune.*

OTHER NOTABLE MILLERS

NICK ALTROCK – Pitcher, 1909--11

Altrock spent nineteen years in the majors, compiling a lifetime record of 84-75 with a 2.67 ERA. He won 20 games three straight years for the White Sox and led the 1906 "Hitless Wonders" to the pennant, then outdueled the Cubs' Three-Finger Brown in the opening game of the World Series, which the White Sox won in six games.

Altrock's best year with the Millers was in 1910, when he worked 300 innings and posted a 19-13 record.

Nick later served as a base coach for the Washington Senators and mixed serious coaching with crowd-pleasing antics. He continued his clowning/coaching into the 1930s.

BELVE BEAN – Pitcher, 1935–40

Bean had a 51-39 record over six years with the Millers. He was later elected Sheriff of Comanche County in Texas and served for eight years.

RUBE BENTON – Pitcher, 1926–33

Notorious for wine and women, Benton won 115 games over eight years for the Millers, including a 20-14 record in 1929. Prior to the Millers, Benton had pitched fifteen years in the National League and was involved in the controversy surrounding the 1919 "Black Sox" scandal. Rube reportedly had advance information that the World Series was fixed and testimony exists that he had won $3,200 betting on Cincinnati in the Series. Benton narrowly escaped disbarment from baseball.

The southpaw was seriously injured in an auto accident in November, 1930. Although his pitching hand was badly crushed, he came back to pitch three more years in Minneapolis. Benton died in 1937 from injuries suffered in another car wreck near Ozark, Arkansas.

MOE BERG – Third baseman-shortstop, 1924

Berg split time with Toledo and Minneapolis in 1924, hitting .264 in 118 games. After he left Minneapolis, he spent fifteen years in the majors, primarily as a catcher.

Probably the most erudite man ever to play professional baseball, Berg accompanied a major-league all-star team to Japan in 1934 and carried out a mission for U. S. intelligence authorities by filming military, industrial, and transportation facilities. Berg's pictures were later used in bombing raids over the Empire, including Jimmy Doolittle's 1942 "Thirty Seconds Over Tokyo" raid.

Berg worked as a spy for the Office of Special Services during World War II. America's top atomic spy, Moe carried out several dangerous missions to determine the Germans' progress toward producing an atomic bomb.

OSSIE BLUEGE – Third baseman-shortstop, 1922.

Ossie hit .315 in 44 games with the Millers in 1922. He then moved to Washington, where he played through 1939, holding down the hot corner for all three Senator pennant-winning teams. Bluege later coached and managed the Senators, then moved into the front office. As a scout, he signed Harmon Killebrew to a Washington contract. He eventually became controller and came with the team when it moved to Minnesota. Bluege retired in 1971, completing a fifty-year career with the Griffith organization.

ED BRESSOUD – Shortstop, 1955-57.

Bressoud hit .251 with 19 home runs and 74 RBIs in 145 games in the Millers' championship season of 1955. He later played 11 seasons in the majors with a .252 lifetime average and 94 home runs.

ORLANDO CEPEDA – First baseman, 1957

Cepeda won the Northern League Triple Crown with the Class-C St. Cloud Rox in 1956, then jumped four classifications and led the Millers with 25 home runs, 108 RBIs and a .309 average the following year.

With the Giants in 1958, Cepeda was the National League Rookie of the Year. In 1967 with St. Louis, the "Baby Bull" was the unanimous selection as the National League's Most Valuable Player.

Surgery on both knees shortened his playing days, and Orlando finished his career as a designated hitter. Still, he compiled a .297 lifetime average in the majors (nine times hitting over. 300) and hit 397 home runs. Cepeda was elected to the Hall of Fame in 1999.

LU CLINTON – Outfielder, 1958-60

Lu led the Millers With 20 home runs in 1959 and added two more in the Junior World Series against Havana. He also hit the Millers' first inside-the-park home run in Met Stadium in July of that year.

Clinton played eight years for five American League teams in the sixties.

ANDY COHEN – Second baseman 1932-39

Cohen came to Minneapolis in a trade with Newark in 1932, played against his former mates in the Junior World Series that fall, and stayed with the Millers through 1939. His best season was in 1934 when he hit .311 and scored 106 runs.

Cohen managed the team for the first 23 games of 1937 because of an illness to Donie Bush. He also hit .320 in 131 games that year.

Andy had played 262 games with the New York Giants during the twenties. He later managed Indianapolis in the American Association and was the head baseball coach at Texas Western College in El Paso for seventeen years.

HUGHIE CRITZ – Second baseman-shortstop, 1923-24

Hughie hit .327 in 1923 with 205 hits, 115 runs scored, and 73 knocked in. He also had a 33-game hitting streak, challenging the league record of 36 at that time, set by Bob Fisher of the Millers in 1921.

Critz was sold to Cincinnati in 1924 and broke into the majors with two hits off Grover Cleveland Alexander. He played twelve seasons in the National League with the Giants and Reds.

JIM DAVENPORT – Third baseman, 1957

Davenport hit .291 in 148 games for the Millers before moving up to the Giants, where he played from 1958 through 1970.

CHARLEY DRESSEN – Third baseman, 1931

Dressen hit .257 in 101 games for the Millers. He had played for the Saints in the early twenties. Dressen later managed Brooklyn, Washington, Milwaukee, and Detroit until his death in August 1966.

PAT DUNCAN – Outfielder, 1925–28

A hard-hitting outfielder who had played seven years in the majors before coming to the Millers, Duncan compiled a .307 lifetime average in the big leagues and appeared in the 1919 World Series with the Cincinnati Reds.

In 1925 with the Millers, Pat hit .345 with 218 hits, 128 runs, 27 homers, and 139 RBI's. He followed that up in 1926 with 23 home runs and 123 RBI's while hitting .351.

FRANK EMMER – Shortstop, 1926–31

Emmer came to the Millers in a trade with Cincinnati in July 1926. The next year he led the Association with 32 home runs while hitting .330. He also drove in 116 runs and scored 154. Emmer broke his ankle in the Millers' 1928 Opener and played in only 64 games that year.

JOE ENGEL – Pitcher, 1915–16

Engel's pitching career, both with the Millers and in the major leagues was brief, but he later became a scout for the Washington Senators and then the longtime owner of the Chattanooga Lookouts in the Southern Association. His predilection for publicity stunts, which included signing a woman and having her pitch to Babe Ruth, Lou Gehrig, and Tony Lazzeri during an exhibition game with the Yankees, earned Engel the title of "Barnum of the Bushes."

TOOKIE GILBERT – First baseman, 1947, 1950–51

A highly-touted prospect, Harold "Tookie" Gilbert may have been picked before he was ripe when he was called up by the New York Giants after only seven games with the Millers in 1950. Failing to make the grade, Gilbert returned to Minneapolis in 1951 and led the Association with 29 home runs. Despite his promise, Tookie never did make much of a splash in the majors. Gilbert died of a heart attack in 1967 at the age of thirty-eight.

ANGELO GIULIANI – Catcher, 1941–42, 1949

Giuliani grew up within sight of the center-field gate of St. Paul's Lexington Park and started his professional career in that city, playing for the Saints from 1932 to 1935. Angie played for the Millers in the early forties, then came out of retirement in 1949 to help out the Millers when injuries left the team short on backstops.

As a catcher for the Washington Senators, Giuliani caught the first game Hall-of-Famer Early Wynn pitched in 1939, and four years later Angie was behind the plate for the last game ever pitched by Hall-of-Famer Lefty Gomez.

Giuliani later became Clinic Director and a scout for the Minnesota Twins. He has performed clinics for over 500,000 youngsters in the upper midwest; as a scout, Giuliani witnessed four of his signees appear in the Twins' Opening Day lineup in 1984.

JOE GLENN – Catcher, 1933

Glenn hit .333 with 17 home runs and 91 RBI's for Minneapolis in 1933. When the Millers' season ended he moved back up to the Yankees and was the catcher when Babe Ruth made his final appearance as a pitcher. Seven years later, Glenn was also the catcher when Ted Williams took the mound for two innings for the Red Sox. Glenn died in his sleep in May 1985, less than twenty-four hours after being inducted into the Pennsylvania Sports Hall of Fame.

HANK GOWDY – Catcher, 1926–27

A seventeen-year veteran in the majors, Gowdy was a member of the 1914 "Miracle Braves" who rose from the cellar in mid-July to win the National League pennant and then swept Connie Mack's A's in the World Series. Gowdy hit .545 in the Series.

Gowdy was the first major-leaguer to enlist in the U. S. Armed Forces during World War I. He saw action at Chateau-Thierry, St. Mihiel, and Argonne, among the bloodiest battles of the war.

PUMPSIE GREEN – Shortstop-second baseman, 1958–59

Green hit .253 for the Millers in 1958 and spent spring training with the Red Sox in 1959. But when Boston sent Green back to the Millers prior to the start of the season, the NAACP in Boston asked a state commission to investigate the employment policy of the Red Sox, who were still the only major-league team who had never had a black on their roster.

The commission eventually cleared the Red Sox of any wrongdoing, and when Green hit .320 for the Millers in 1959 and was named to the Association All-Star team, he was called up by the Red Sox in late July as Boston became final team in the majors to integrate.

JACK HARSHMAN – First baseman-pitcher, 1949–50, 1952

Harshman hit 40 home runs for the Millers in 1949, but in 1950, while playing for Jacksonville, he got a chance to pitch for the first time. And even though Jack hit 47 homers for Nashville of the Southern Association in 1951, he came back to the Millers as a pitcher the following year. On the mound, he posted a 6-7 record and threw a one-hitter against Kansas City in the playoffs.

Harshman compiled a lifetime record of 69-65 in the majors.

CLINT HARTUNG – Pitcher-outfielder, 1942, 1952–53

Mike Kelley signed Hartung out of Hondo High School in Texas in 1942, had him pitch briefly for the Millers, then shipped him off to Eau Claire to work under the tutelage of manager Rosy Ryan.

When he returned to the Millers ten years later, after spending time in the majors, he was an outfielder. The "Hondo Hurricane" hit .334 for the Millers with 27 home runs and 93 RBI's in 1952. The following year he hit two home runs in one inning, both in excess of 425 feet.

Hartung never fulfilled his potential in the majors, either as a pitcher or a slugger.

WILLIE KIRKLAND – Outfielder, 1955–56

Kirkland joined the Millers near the end of the 1955 season after hitting 40 home runs for Sioux City in the Western League. In 1956 Willie hit .293 with 37 home runs and 120 RBI's.

Kirkland later compiled a .240 average with 148 home runs in nine seasons in the majors.

DAN LALLY – Outfielder, 1895–98, 1900, 1902–04

Lally played with Miller teams in the Western League, American League and American Association. In 1895 Dan hit .400 with 36 home runs. He also scored 205 runs that year, which only tied him for the league lead in that department.

AD LISKA – Pitcher, 1928, 1932

Liska won nine straight games for the Millers in 1928 en route a 20-4 record with 3.68 ERA in 225 innings pitched.

PAT MALONE – Pitcher, 1924–25, 1927

Malone won 20 games for the Millers while working 319 innings in 1927. He later pitched in two World Series for the Cubs and one for the Yankees (Joe McCarthy was his manager for both teams.)

Malone twice won 20 games for the Cubs and had a 134-92 record in ten seasons in the majors.

DAVE MANN – Outfielder, 1960

Mann led the American Association with 50 stolen bases in 1960. The swift switch-hitter never made the majors, but did lead various minor leagues in stolen bases nine times.

BOB MEUSEL – Outfielder, 1931

A big gun on the Yankees' Murderers' Row in the twenties, Meusel led the American League in home runs and RBI's in 1925, and hit .309 with 156 home runs during his eleven-year career in the majors.

Meusel played in 59 games with the Millers, hitting .283. In one game in July 1931 he had four hits, including a grand slam, and knocked in seven runs.

JIM MIDDLETON – Pitcher, 1925–27, 1929

Middleton was thirty-six years old when he won ten-straight games for the Millers in 1925. The next year he was a 20-game winner. His four-year record with the Millers was 54-38, even though he consistently walked more batters than he struck out each year.

BILL MONBOUQUETTE – Pitcher, 1958

Monbo was 8-9 with the Millers in 1958. Highlights of his eleven-year career in the majors include a 20-win season for the Red Sox in 1963, a no-hitter against the White Sox in 1962, and a game in 1961 in which he struck out 17 batters.

VAN LINGLE MUNGO – Pitcher, 1942

A hard-throwing, hard-living righthander with the Brooklyn Dodgers in the thirties, Van Lingle Mungo's blazing fastball, once clocked at over 100 miles per hour, was gone by the time he joined the Millers. After arm surgery in 1940, Mungo relied on a spitter and other off-speed deliveries.

He was 11-3 for the Minneapolis in 1942 before he was sold to the Giants in late July. Millers' teammate Bill Barnacle recalled that Mungo was a loner and didn't associate with anyone on the team. Barnacle also reports that Mungo "would occasionally disappear for several days, but always rejoined the team someplace."

FRED OLMSTEAD – Pitcher, 1908–13

Olmstead pitched nine shutouts and won 24 games in 1909 despite missing the final month of the season when he was sold to the White Sox. The right-handed spitballer led the Association in wins in 1912 and finished with a 28-10 record.

ERNIE ORSATTI – Outfielder, 1928

Off the field, Orsatti worked as a Hollywood stunt man for many actors, most notably Buster Keaton.

On the field, Orsatti was the property of the St. Louis Cardinals. He was farmed out to Minneapolis and burned up the American Association with a .381 average in 123 games in 1928, but was recalled by the Cards in August. Mike Kelley blames the Millers' failure to win the 1928 pennant on the recall of Orsatti.

YIP OWENS – Catcher, 1910–13, 1916–20, 1922

A durable catcher and clubhouse prankster, Frank "Yip" Owens played ten seasons in Minneapolis, the longest tenure of any Miller catcher.

Owens had played for Boston and Chicago in the American League before coming to the Millers. He also played for Brooklyn and Baltimore in the Federal League in 1914–15.

Following his career, Owens lived in Minneapolis until his death in 1958.

ROY PATTERSON – Pitcher, 1908–1914, 1917–19

The spitballing righthander was a 20-game winner for the Millers in 1908, 1910, 1911, and 1912. He returned to Minneapolis to help a thinned-out mound staff during World War I and pitched three more years. His ten-year record with the Millers was 135-73.

In 1908 Patterson outdueled Indianapolis's Rube Marquard, beating the future Hall-of-Famer, 1-0, in 11 innings. Two years later, Roy relieved a Miller starter in the first and pitched the final 17 2/3 innings for a 3-2 win over St. Paul.

Patterson pitched for the Chicago White Sox from 1901–07. He won 20 games for the Sox in 1901 and also delivered the first pitch for the American League when it became a major league. (The batter he first pitched to was Ollie Pickering, who would later be a teammate of Patterson on the Millers.)

JESS PETTY – Pitcher, 1932–35

The Silver Fox was thirty-eight when he joined the Millers and posted records of 16-10, 18-8 and 19-7 in his first three years with the team.

Petty fanned 11 and pitched a five-hitter in beating Newark, 3-2, in the second game of the 1932 Junior World Series.

ROY PFLEGER – Outfielder, 1936–39

A left-handed hitter who never made the majors, Pfleger hit 87 home runs in 472 games with Minneapolis and twice drove in more than 100 runs in a season.

Pfleger led the Association with 29 home runs in 1937. The year before, he hit two home runs, including a grand slam, in one inning.

DEACON PHILLIPPE – Pitcher 1897–98

Phillipe spent his only two years in the minor leagues with the Millers, winning 21 games for them in 1898. He then embarked on a thirteen-year career in the National League, winning 186 games and losing 110.

For Pittsburgh in the 1903 World Series, Deacon pitched five complete games and won three of them. Despite his efforts, the Pirates were beaten in the Series by Boston, five games to three.

DICK RADATZ – Pitcher, 1960

A 1959 graduate of Michigan State, Radatz had a 3-0 record for the Millers in 1960 and was the starting pitcher in the final game ever played by the Millers, September 11, 1960. He was converted into a relief pitcher the following year at Seattle, then moved up to the Boston Red Sox.

The six foot-six righthander with the 95 mile per hour fastball was nicknamed "The Monster" as he twice led the American League in saves in the early sixties.

FLINT RHEM – Pitcher, 1929

Much was expected from Rhem in 1929, but he could only produce a 5-11 record with a 5.40 ERA for the Millers.

A drinking companion of Grover Cleveland Alexander's in St. Louis, Rhem once failed to show up for a game for the Cardinals. Upon his return to the team, he claimed he had been kidnapped and forced by his abductors to consume large quantities of whiskey.

PAUL RICHARDS – Catcher 1932

Richards hit .361 with 16 home runs and 69 RBI's in only 78 games with the Millers.

Richards gained fame in the fifties and sixties as an innovative General Manager with the Baltimore Orioles, Houston Colts, and Atlanta Braves. He had managed the White Sox to four consecutive winning seasons starting in 1951 and was later lured out of retirement by Bill Veeck in 1976 to manage the White Sox at the age of sixty-seven.

HENRI RONDEAU – Outfielder-catcher, 1913–24

Rondeau spent twelve years with the Millers, longer than any other player. He hit over .300 seven of those years.

ROSY RYAN – Pitcher, 1932, 1934–36

Rosy Ryan pitched ten years in the majors, five of them with the New York Giants. In 1922 he led the National League in ERA, and in three World Series with the Giants, he posted a 3-0 record (all of his wins coming in relief). In 1924 he also became the first National League pitcher to hit a home run in the World Series.

Rosy came to Minneapolis in 1932. As he had in the majors, Ryan worked primarily as a reliever, but still tied for the Association lead with 22 victories in 1932. He had an 11-5 record with the 1935 Millers, but missed most of the 1936 season following an appendectomy.

Ryan came back to manage the Millers in 1944 and 1945, then became their General Manager for twelve years and continued in the post for another ten years when the team was shifted to Phoenix. Ryan died of cancer in 1982.

CARL SAWATSKI – Catcher 1955

A burly catcher who hit .268 with 27 home runs for the Millers' championship team in 1955, Sawatski played with four National League teams between 1948 and 1963.

Sawatski later became a minor-league executive and has served as president of the Texas League since 1970.

RUBE SCHAUER – 1919,1921-23

Born Dimitri Ivanovich Dimitrihoff, the native of Odessa, Russia won his first nine games with the Millers in 1919. He finished the season with a 21-17 record and a 2.64 ERA in 351 innings pitched.

CHUCK SCHILLING – Second baseman, 1959-60

Schilling hit .314 in 142 games for the Millers in 1960. He played five years for the Red Sox after that and had a .239 lifetime batting average.

FRANK SHELLENBACK – Pitcher, 1918-19

In both 1918 and 1919 Shellenback split time between the Millers and Chicago @te Sox. Dependent on a spitball, he was not able to return to the majors when the spitter was outlawed in 1920. Instead, he pitched nineteen seasons in the Pacific Coast League and won 315 games in his minor-league career. In 1948 he returned to Minneapolis to manage the Millers.

ROY SMALLEY – Shortstop, 1959

The brother-in-law of manager Gene Mauch, Smalley came to the Millers from Houston midway through the 1959 season. He hit only .236 that year, but hit a two-run homer in the second game of the Junior World Series against Havana.

Smalley had played eleven years with the Cubs, Braves and Phillies.

EARL SMITH – Outfielder, 1922,1924-30

The switch-hitting outfielder knocked in more than 100 runs five times with the Millers. In 1924 he hit .353 while scoring 139 runs. The following year he hit 31 home runs and drove in 156.

ERNIE SMITH – Shortstop, 1930-34

Smith hit .314 in 647 games with the Millers over five years. He scored 108 runs and drove in 111 in helping the Millers to the 1932 pennant.

TRACY STALLARD – Pitcher, 1959-60

Stallard, who had a 9-16 record in his two years with the Millers, is best remembered for giving up Roger Maris's 61st home run in 1961.

CHUCK TANNER – Outfielder, 1959

In 1955 Chuck Tanner homered in his first at-bat in the majors. In the 1959 season opener, he homered in his first at-bat in a Millers' uniform. In the Millers' home opener that year, Tanner again homered in his first at-bat. Chuck hit .319 for the Millers that year and led the Association in doubles.

Tanner later managed four clubs in the majors. In 1972, while with the White Sox, he was named American League Manager of the Year; in 1979, he led the Pirates to the World Championship.

WALLY TAUSCHER – Pitcher, 1933-41

Tauscher had 133-78 record in nine years with the Millers, including a 21-7 record in 1934.

BOB TILLMAN – Catcher, 1960

Tillman led the Millers with 24 home runs and 82 RBIs, and was the starting catcher in the 1960 Association All-Star game. Tillman played with the Red Sox, Yankees, and Braves from 1962-70.

FRANK TRECHOCK – Second baseman-shortstop, 1940–41, 1943, 1946–48

Trechock played in only one major-league game, but he held down the middle infield for the Millers through the forties. He left the team to join the Army in August 1943, but rejoined the Millers after the war and hit .290 in both 1946 and 1947.

BROADWAY CHARLIE WAGNER – Pitcher, 1937–38

Nicknamed "Broadway" because of his good looks and extravagant wardrobe, Wagner was a 20-game winner for the Millers in 1937.

WES WESTRUM – Catcher, 1941–42, 1947

Westrum appeared in only one game for the Millers in 1941 and three games in 1942, but returned in 1947 to hit .294 with 22 home runs and 87 RBI's.

A native of Clearbrook, Minnesota, Westrum hit only .217 lifetime in the majors, but his defensive skills kept him in the big leagues for eleven seasons. In 1950 he led National League catchers in assists and double plays.

Westrum replaced Casey Stengel as manager of the Mets in 1965 and later managed the Giants. He is still active in the game as a scout for the Atlanta Braves.

JIMMY WILLIAMS – Second baseman, 1910–15

Williams hit .275 in a major-league career that lasted from 1899 to 1909. Three times he was the league leader in triples. He then joined the Millers for their championship years under the Cantillons. Twice he hit over .300 and in 1913 appeared in 172 games.

EARL WILSON – Pitcher, 1959–60

Wilson struck out 246 batters in 225 innings in his two years with the Millers. He was called up by the Red Sox in July both years, but had enough time in 1959 to win nine straight games and be named to the Association All-Star team.

Wilson pitched a no-hitter for the Red Sox in 1962 and led the American League, while pitching for Detroit, with 22 wins in 1967.

Chuck Tanner connecting for a home run at Met Stadium.
Minneapolis Star and Tribune.

APPENDIX

MINNEAPOLIS MILLERS
AMERICAN ASSOCIATION
1902–1960

Year	Won	Lost	Place	Manager	Attendance
1902	54	86	Seventh	Walter Wilmot	
1903	50	91	Seventh	Wilmot-George Yeager	
1904	78	67	Fourth	W. H. Watkins	
1905	88	62	Third	W. H. Watkins	
1906	79	66	Third	Mike Kelley	
1907	80	74	Third	Mike Cantillon	
1908	77	77	Fifth	Mike Cantillon	125,203
1909	88	79	Third	Jimmy Collins	217,130
1910	107	61	First	Joe Cantillon	195,058
1911	99	66	First	Joe Cantillon	208,588
1912	105	60	First	Joe Cantillon	198,005
1913	97	70	Second	Joe Cantillon	175,046
1914	75	93	Seventh	Joe Cantillon	104,975
1915	92	62	First	Joe Cantillon	149,931
1916	88	76	Third	Joe Cantillon	131,627
1917	68	86	Sixth	Joe Cantillon	88,138
1918	34	42	Seventh	Joe Cantillon	
1919	72	82	Fifth	Joe Cantillon	108,459
1920	85	79	Fourth	Joe Cantillon	223,671
1921	92	73	Second	Joe Cantillon	273,159
1922	92	75	Second	Joe Cantillon	225,523
1923	74	92	Sixth	Joe Cantillon	165,643
1924	77	89	Sixth	Mike Kelley	181,094
1925	86	80	Fourth	Mike Kelley	233,065
1926	72	94	Seventh	Mike Kelley	177,626
1927	88	80	Fifth	Mike Kelley	185,363
1928	97	71	Second	Mike Kelley	252,875
1929	89	78	Third	Mike Kelley	187,246
1930	77	76	Fourth	Mike Kelley	184,116

MINNEAPOLIS MILLERS
AMERICAN ASSOCIATION
1902–1960

Year	Won	Lost	Place	Manager	Attendance
1931	80	88	Sixth	Mike Kelley	132,740
1932	100	68	First	Donie Bush	204,567
1933	86	67	Second	Dave Bancroft	151,808
1934	85	64	First	Donie Bush	164,390
1935	91	63	First	Donie Bush	161,036
1936	78	76	Fifth	Donie Bush	142,926
1937	87	67	Third	Donie Bush	193,898
1938	78	74	Sixth	Donie Bush	181,681
1939	99	55	Second	Tom Sheehan	210,082
1940	86	59	Third	Tom Sheehan	155,523
1941	83	70	Fourth	Tom Sheehan	118,707
1942	76	78	Seventh	Tom Sheehan	112,304
1943	67	84	Sixth	Tom Sheehan	90,904
1944	54	97	Seventh	Rosy Ryan	82,759
1945	72	81	Fifth	Rosy Ryan	122,376
1946	76	75	Fourth	Zeke Bonura-Ryan-Sheehan	242,603
1947	77	77	Fourth	Tom Sheehan	273,253
1948	77	77	Fifth	Frank Shellenback-Chick Genovese-Billy Herman	274,890
1949	74	78	Fourth	Tommy Heath	247,637
1950	90	64	First	Tommy Heath	238,285
1951	77	75	Fifth	Tommy Heath	143,279
1952	79	75	Fourth	Chick Genovese	120,185
1953	76	78	Fifth	Genovese-Fred Fitzsimmons	128,630
1954	78	73	Third	Bill Rigney	128,187
1955	92	62	First	Bill Rigney	168,697
1956	78	74	Fourth	Eddie Stanky	318,326
1957	85	69	Third	Red Davis	256,113
1958	82	71	Third	Gene Mauch	152,533
1959	95	67	Second	Gene Mauch	160,167
1960	82	72	Fifth	Eddie Popowski	115,702

MINNEAPOLIS MILLERS
1902–1960

HOME RUN LEADERS

1907	John (Buck) Freeman	18
1908	John (Buck) Freeman	10 (tie)
1910	Gavvy Cravath	14
1911	Gavvy Cravath	29
1923	Carlton East	31
1927	Frank Emmer	32
1928	Spencer Harris	32
1930	Nick Cullop	54
1932	Joe Hauser	49
1933	Joe Hauser	69
1934	Buzz Arlett	41
1935	John Gill	43
1937	Roy Pfleger	29
1938	Ted Williams	43
1940	Ab Wright	39
1941	Ab Wright	26
1944	Babe Barna	24
1945	Babe Barna	25
1949	Charlie Workman	41
1951	Tookie Gilbert	29
1953	George Wilson	34

BATTING CHAMPIONS

1909	Tip O'Neill	.296
1910	Gavvy Cravath	.326
1911	Gavvy Cravath	.363
1932	Art Ruble	.376
1938	Ted Williams	.366
1940	Ab Wright	.343
1955	Rance Pless	.337

RBI LEADERS (Since 1920)

1926	Pat Duncan	123
1930	Nick Cullop	152
1932	Babe Ganzel	143
1933	Joe Hauser	182
1935	John Gill	154
1937	Ralph (Red) Kress	157
1938	Ted Williams	142
1940	Ab Wright	159
1946	John McCarthy	122

LEADERS IN PITCHING VICTORIES

1910	Tom Hughes	31
1911	Roy Patterson	24
1912	Fred Olmstead	28
1915	Mutt Williams	29
1916	Earl Yingling	24
1931	Dutch Henry	23
1932	Rosy Ryan	22 (tie)
1934	Wally Tauscher	21
1939	Herb Hash	22
1955	Al Worthington	19
1956	Curt Barclay	15 (tie)

NO-HITTERS BY MILLERS

Date	Pitcher	Opponent	Score
August 2, 1912	Bill Lelivelt	Toledo	4-0
May 19, 1915	Harry Harper	St. Paul	4-0
May 26, 1940	Mickey Haefner	Milwaukee	4-0 (6 innings)
June 10, 1948	Monte Kennedy	Louisville	14-0
July 27, 1950	Kirby Higbe	Columbus	3-1 (7 innings)
August 10, 1950	Dixie Howell	Columbus	6-0
* April 16, 1957	Stu Miller	Indianapolis	1-0 (6 innings)

* Season Opener

MILLERS AS HOST OF AMERICAN ASSOCIATION ALL-STAR GAME

July 19, 1934   Minneapolis 13   All-Stars 6
Winning pitcher–Tiny Chaplin
Losing pitcher–Gene Trow (St. Paul)

July 30, 1935   Minneapolis 4   All-Stars 3
Winning pitcher–Steve Sundra
Losing pitcher–Garland Braxton (Milwaukee)

July 16, 1941   All-Stars 6   Minneapolis 1
Winning pitcher–Ray Starr (Indianapolis)
Losing pitcher–Chief Hogsett

July 21, 1955   All-Stars 16   Minneapolis 6
Winning pitcher–Don Larsen (Denver)
Losing pitcher–Ralph Branca

July 13, 1959   Minneapolis 2   All-Stars 0
Winning pitcher–Chet Nichols
Losing pitcher–Ed Donnelly (Denver)

MINNEAPOLIS MILLERS
IN HALL OF FAME
(Years with team in parentheses)

	Year of Induction
Roger Bresnahan (1898-99)	1945
Jimmy Collins (Player-manager 1909)	1945
Rube Waddell (1911-13)	1946
Urban (Red) Faber (1911)	1964
Bill McKechnie (1921)	1962
Zack Wheat (1928)	1959
George Kelly (1930-31)	1973
Ted Williams (1938)	1966
Billy Herman (Player-manager 1948)	1975
Ray Dandridge (1949-52)	1987
Hoyt Wilhelm (1950-51)	1985
Willie Mays (1951)	1979
Monte Irvin (1955)	1973
Orlando Cepeda (1957)	1999
Carl Yastrzemski (1959-60)	1989
Dave Bancroft (Manager 1933)	1971
Jimmie Foxx (Coach 1958)	1951

JOE HAUSER
1933 HOME RUNS

HR No.	Game No.	Date	Opponent	Score	Pitcher	Inning	Men On Base
1	10	4/27	Toledo	13–8	Monte Pearson-R	1	2
2	11	4/28	Toledo	15–11	Roxie Lawson-R	1	2
3	11	4/28			Roxie Lawson-R	3	3
4	11	4/28			Ralph Winegarner-R	8	0
5	15	5/ 3	Columbus	7–8	Paul Dean-R	3	2
6	15	5/ 3			Paul Dean-R	5	1
7	17	5/ 6	Indianapolis	11–10	Bill Thomas-R	2	0
8	18	5/10	Louisville	10–9 (10)	Archie McKain-L	6	0
9	19	5/11–1	Louisville	4–6	Johnny Marcum-R	3	0
10	23	5/14	at St. Paul	15–5	Floyd Newkirk-R	6	0
11	32	5/23	Milwaukee	19–5	Americo Polli-R	1	2
12	32	5/23			Harold Hillin-R	7	1
13	33	5/24	Milwaukee	5–8	Garland Braxton-L	8	1
14	35	5/26	Kansas City	9–3	Joe Blackwell-L	1	1
15	35	5/26			Joe Blackwell-L	3	0
16	38	5/30pm	St. Paul	7–6 (10)	Les Munns-R	9	0
17	39	5/31	at St. Paul	6–1	Floye Newkirk-R	1	1
18	41	6/ 3	at Columbus	1–5	Bill Lee-R	9	0
19	43	6/ 4–2	at Columbus	7–9	Jim Lindsey-R	1	0
20	43	6/ 4–2			Jim Lindsey-R	4	1
21	49	6/ 8–2	at Toledo	7–10	Forrest Twogood-L	4	0
22	49	6/ 8–2			Ralph Winegarner-R	9	0
23	52	6/10	at Indianapolis	4–3 (10)	Bill Thomas-R	10	0
24	57	6/13–2	at Louisville	9–13	Phil Weinert-L	1	1
25	58	6/14n	at Louisville	7–6	Archie McKain-L	5	0
26	62	6/21–1	at Milwaukee	5–7	Garland Braxton-L	6	1
27	67	6/25–1	St. Paul	3–5	Emil Yde-L	5	0
28	68	6/25–2	St. Paul	10–1	Les Munns-R	3	0
29	68	6/25–2			Less Munns-R	4	1
30	69	6/26	Kansas City	10–6	Lou Fette-R	5	0
30	71	6/28	Kansas City	4–3 (10)	Duster Mails-L	6	0
32	72	6/29	Milwaukee	9–8 (10)	Garland Braxton-L	9	0
33	82	7/ 9–1	Toledo	9–12	Roxie Lawson-R	1	1
34	82	7/ 9–1			Forrest Twogood-L	7	0
35	83	7/ 9–2	Toledo	8–3	Thornton Lee-L	3	0
36	84	7/10	Columbus	8–6	Clarence Heise-L	3	1

JOE HAUSER
1933 HOME RUNS

HR No.	Game No.	Date	Opponent	Score	Pitcher	Inning	Men On Base
37	85	7/11	Columbus	14–6	Bud Teachout-L	3	0
38	85	7/11			Bud Teachout-L	4	3
39	86	7/12	Columbus	5–7	Bill Lee-R	6	1
40	87	7/13	Columbus	10–9	Clarence Heise-L	8	0
41	88	7/14–1	Louisville	8–2	Clyde Hatter-L	7	1
42	92	7/16–2	Louisville	8–6	Johnny Marcum-R	1	1
43	93	7/17	Indianapolis	5–10	Stew Bolen-L	6	0
44	95	7/19–1	Indianapolis	7–5	Stew Bolen-L	9	3
45	97	7/20	Indianapolis	8–9 (10)	Stew Bolen-L	7	0
46	98	7/21	Milwaukee	7–6	Fred Stiely-L	1	2
47	99	7/22	Milwaukee	13–9	Harold Hillin-R	4	1
48	100	7/23–1	Milwaukee	7–8	Garland Braxton-L	1	1
49	100	7/23–1			Garland Braxton-L	3	0
50	105	7/27–1	at Milwaukee	11–8	Harold Hillin-R	9	0
51	107	7/28	at Milwaukee	6–5	Garland Braxton-L	8	0
52	110	7/30–2	at Kansas City	15–2	Joe Blackwell-L	3	0
53	114	8/ 5–1	at Indianapolis	3–10	Stew Bolen-L	8	1
54	124	8/12	at Toledo	8–4	Forrest Twogood-L	3	0
55	125	8/13–1	at Toledo	3–0	Ralph Winegarner-R	5	0
56	128	8/15	Louisville	13–6	Clyde Hatter-L	4	2
57	129	8/16	Louisville	16–1	Dick Bass-R	4	1
58	130	8/17	Louisville	5–8	Ken Penner-R	3	0
59	131	8/18	Indianapolis	11–6	Jim Turner-R	6	0
60	134	8/20–2	Indianapolis	14–6	Bill Thomas-R	7	1
61	138	8/24	Toledo	15–8	Ralph Winegarner-R	5	0
62	140	8/26	Columbus	8–6	Bill Lee-R	3	1
63	148	9/ 4am	at St. Paul	5–3	Les Munns-R	7	0
64	148	9/ 4am			Les Munns-R	9	0
65	149	9/ 4pm	St. Paul	5–11	Floyd Newkirk-R	2	1
66	151	9/ 7	Milwaukee	8–7	Paul Gregory-R	1	1
67	152	9/ 8	Milwaukee	7–3	Forest Pressnell-R	4	1
68	153	9/ 9	Kansas City	6–8	Duster Mails-L	4	0
69	153	9/ 9			Duster Mails-L	9	2

SOURCES

Library files of the *Minneapolis Tribune, Minneapolis Star, Minneapolis Journal, St. Paul Dispatch, St. Paul Pioneer Press, New York Times, Milwaukee Journal.*

Society for American Baseball Research (SABR) private collections of *The Sporting News, Sporting Life.*

Alexander, Charles C. *Ty Cobb.* New York: Oxford University Press, 1984.

Allen, Lee. *The American League Story.* New York: Hill and Wang, 1962.

All-Time Records and Highlights of the American Association. Wichita: American Association, 1971.

Barton, George A. *My Lifetime in Sports.* Minneapolis: Olympic Press, 1957.

Baseball Encyclopedia, The. New York: MacMillan, 1979.

Baseball Historical Review. Cooperstown, NY: SABR, 1981.

Baseball Research Journal. Cooperstown, NY: SABR, 1975, 1977, 1978, 1979, 1980, 1981, 1982, 1983,1984,1985,1986.

Cepeda, Orlando with Bob Markus. *High & Inside.* South Bend, IN: Icarus Press, 1983.

Dickey, Glenn. *The History of National League Baseball.* New York: Stein and Day, 1979.

Finch, Robert L., Addington, L. H., and Morgan, Ben M., ed. *The Story of Minor League Baseball.* Columbus: The National Association of Professional Baseball Leagues, 1952.

French, Robert A. *50 Golden Years in the American Association.* Minneapolis: Syndicate Printing, 1951.

Holway, John. *Voices from the Great Black Baseball Leagues.* New York: Dodd and Mead, 1975.

James, Bill. The Bill James Historical Baseball Abstract. New York: Villard Books, 1985. Karst, Gene and Jones, Martin J. *Who's Who in Professional Baseball.* New Rochelle, NY:

Arlington House, 1973.

Kaufman, Louis; Fitzgerald, Barbara; and Sewall, Tom. *Moe Berg: Athlete, Scholar. . . Spy.* Boston: Little, Brown and Company, 1974.

MacFarlan, Paul, ed. *Daguerreotypes.* St. Louis: The Sporting News, 1981.

Mayer, Ronald A. *The 1937 Newark Bears.* Union City, NJ: William H. Wise and Co., 1980.

Minor League Baseball Stars, vols. 1 and 2. Cooperstown, NY: SABR, 1978 and 1985.

Murdock, Eugene C. *Ban Johnson: Czar of Baseball.* Westport, CT: Greenwood Press, 1982.

O'Connor, Leslie M., ed. *Official Baseball.* New York: A. S. Barnes and Co., 1946. *Official Baseball Guide.* St. Louis: The Sporting News, 1942, 1943, 1944, 1945, 1946, 1947, 1948, 1949, 1950, 1951,

SOURCES

1952, 1953, 1954, 1955, 1956, 1957,1958,1959,1960,1961.

Peterson, Robert. Only the Ball was White. New York: McGraw-Hill, 1970.

Reach Official Base Ball Guide, The. Philadelphia: A. J. Reach Company, 1905, 1909, 1910, 1914, 1915, 1920, 1924, 1925, 1927, 1928, 1940, 1941.

Rogosin, Donn. Invisible Men: Life in Baseball's Negro Leagues. New York: Atheneum, 1983.

Spalding's Official Base Ball Guide. New York: American Sports Publishing Co., 1901, 1905, 1906, 1907, 1908, 1909, 1910, 1911, 1912, 1913, 1914, 1915, 1916, 1917, 1918, 1919, 1920, 1921, 1922, 1923, 1926, 1929, 1930, 1931, 1932, 1933, 1934, 1935, 1936, 1937, 1938, 1939, 1940, 1941.

Veeck, Bill with Ed Linn. Veeck – as in Wreck. New York: G. P. Putnam's Sons, 1962.

Williams, Ted. My Turn at Bat: The Story of My Life. New York: Pocket Books, 1969. Index

Index